MY FATHER AND I

AND I

How the Bible Teaches Fatherhood

by

Judson Cornwall

McDougal Publishing is a ministry of The McDougal Foundation, Inc., a Maryland nonprofit corporation dedicated to spreading the Gospel of the Lord Jesus Christ to as many people as possible in the shortest time possible.

Published by:

McDougal Publishing
P.O. Box 3595
Hagerstown, MD 21742-3595

ISBN 1-884369-78-2

Printed in the United States of America
For Worldwide Distribution

DEDICATION

I dedicate this book to my three daughters–Dorothy Cornwall, Jeannie Miller, and Justine Senftleben– who taught me the great joy and privilege of being a father. They survived beautifully in spite of my inexperience.

Contents

PREFACE

Several years ago my brother Robert asked me, "Judson, give me a good Bible role model for a father," and I found that I couldn't. The thought continued to surface in my mind until it developed into a Father's Day sermon the next year. A few months later I was asked to write four articles on being a father for a magazine, and I enlarged on that sermon. A publisher saw those articles and asked me to expand them into a book. And this is it.

Being a father used to go along with getting married, but not anymore. Although there were over four million live births in America during 1994, fatherhood is on the decline in the United States. Less than half of the nation's 68.1 million families had children present in the home in 1993. Two-parent families accounted for only thirty-six percent of family households in that year, down from fifty percent in 1970. Nearly a third of all family groups with children were maintained by single parents in 1993. A high proportion of couples are using birth control, and abandonment and divorce have deprived many children of a resident father.

Whatever reasons a man may have that cause him to sidestep the responsibilities of being a father, he is not cheating only his wife and children; he is cheating himself out of one of God's most wonderful and maturing experiences.

God's emphasis on the family is underscored when we realize that the Bible speaks of family or families 299 times in 238 verses. It refers to mother or mothers 253 times in 233 verses, children 1,802 times in 1,515 verses, and to father or fathers 1,528 times in 1,366 verses. No Bible doctrine is alluded to as frequently as these units of the home. Having children is God's will, plan, and purpose for His creatures.

Today's generation seems to have little teaching on how to fulfill the role of the father. It is my hope that this book will help fill that need and inspire men to be the best possible father to their children. Children are a gift from the Lord, an incomparable heritage, and a perpetual source of inspiration, joy, and challenge. No father will ever suffer from boredom!

INTRODUCTION

God has blessed me with three daughters, and those precious daughters have given me five granddaughters and four grandsons. These, in turn, have given me thirteen great-grandchildren, almost equally split between sons and daughters. And nothing in life has given me more pleasure than being a father, a father-in-law, a grandfather and a great-grandfather.

It troubles me, therefore, when I see the reluctance and, many times, the sheer dread of modern men when they are faced with the prospect of having to assume this role of fatherhood. It is a God-given privilege to be a father, a privilege each of us should joyfully embrace when it comes our way.

To all those who are experiencing mixed emotions about the prospect of fatherhood, I dedicate the teachings of this book, borne of my own joyful experiences. May God grant you the insight to know His will for you in this regard, that you may not miss one of the very best blessings He has reserved for you.

Judson Cornwall
1997

Whoever has my commands and obeys them, he is the one who loves me. He who loves me will be loved by my Father, and I too will love him and show myself to him.
                                        John 14:21

ACCEPTING THE ROLE OF FATHER

My Father, who has given them to me, is greater than all; no one can snatch them out of my Father's hand.   John 10:29

"Honey, the doctor says I'm pregnant!"

This announcement can induce fear into a man faster than a registered letter from the IRS, especially if it's a first pregnancy. The man often stares unbelievingly at his wife while his mind races a mile a minute:

"We're going to have a baby!"

"I'm going to be a father!"

"Me—a father? I don't know how to be a father!"

Whether he feels elated or exasperated, I can almost guarantee that he feels afraid. He may have barely gotten used to sharing his life with his wife, and now he must further share it with a baby. It is the end of his monopoly on his wife's affections, time and energy. The baby will command those things from her for many years to come.

The birth of a child forces changes that will be lifelong and constantly challenging. This new father faces the dilemma of being the provider, protector, instructor, and a hundred other things to this child. It will be a lifetime responsibility with ever-changing roles. He will barely get comfortable in one role before it changes, as he progressively moves from husband to father, to father-in-law, to grandfather, to great-grandfather.

This stunned young man may lift Paul's statement out of context and apply it to himself: *"Who is equal to such a task?"* (2 Corinthians 2:16). At the moment, he certainly does not feel up to this new role.

The friends of this father-to-be don't know whether to congratulate him or commiserate with him. These are not easy times in which to fill the role of a father. It has become a very nebulous role today. More and more women choose to have babies without getting married, and nearly half of all marriages end in divorce. This leads many men to believe that they are necessary for siring a child, but nonessential for the raising of that child. More than thirty percent of American homes with children don't have a resident father.

Has fatherhood gone out of style? Or is it just too difficult for our soft American lifestyle?

There are far more American men who can embrace a woman than can embrace the responsibilities of fatherhood. A wife's announcement of pregnancy challenges the husband's inherent selfishness. The world will no longer revolve around him, and the baby will become the focus of the home. Dad must either step aside and give place to the baby or run from the responsibilities of fatherhood.

OPTIONS AVAILABLE

"Did you hear what I said? I said we're going to have a baby," the wife repeats.

During premarital counseling he had been reminded that plans for marriage are plans for a family. At the altar, when he accepted his bride as his lifelong companion, he may also have been asked whether he would accept any children the Lord should bless them with. He had mentally accepted children as fact, but now the reality of that aspect of marriage is pressing almost painfully upon him. They probably hadn't planned for this—at least not yet.

The man's mind reaches for options. Basically, there are but four options available to him:

1. Abandon the marriage.
2. Abort the baby.
3. Adopt the baby out.
4. Accept his parental responsibilities.

ABANDONING THE MARRIAGE

Far too many American men grab the first option and abandon the marriage as quickly as possible.

Their selfish nature is unwilling to share with a baby. Their immaturity and self-centeredness demand that they remain number one. One evening, the husband just doesn't come home and, frequently, the wife never hears from him again. What should have been the most joyous experience since their joining in marriage becomes a tragedy for the mother-to-be. Her man has bailed out of his role of fatherhood.

Now this pregnant wife faces not only the coming of a new life that will be completely dependent upon her, but also the loss of her source of income, emotional strength, and partner in child-raising. She encounters the challenge of being a single parent.

She will not be alone. According to the 1995 *World Almanac*, nearly 30 percent of all family groups with children were maintained by single parents— mostly women [1]. This indicates that nearly a third of fathers abandon their family responsibilities by desertion or divorce.

ABORTING THE UNBORN CHILD

It is unlikely that you would be reading this book if you intended to abandon your wife and coming child. I seriously hope you are not considering abortion either, even though it is legal and common in America. In the United States during 1992, more than one and a half million babies who were conceived were not allowed to gestate to full term. They were medically and legally "terminated." In many cases they were conceived but flushed out of the mother's womb by a birth control method that prevents implantation, and the mother (and father) never even knew she was pregnant.

What you may not know is that abortion is decisively condemned in the Bible. Although surgical abortion was not as common in Bible times as it is today, chemical or herbal abortions were common enough that Hippocrates, around 400 B.C., included in his oath a pledge to never give a woman any drug to induce abortion.

The ancient Israelites also, in their apostasy, practiced the killing of their newborn children in a way that presents a chilling parallel to the modern "partial birth" abortions, in which the child is killed even while being born. The Israelites allowed the child to be born and then offered the baby to the fire god Molech. It was quite a religious ceremony performed at high feast days to the accompaniment of drums and music. While the parents worshiped Molech, the priests of Molech threw the baby into a raging fire. The pulsating drums drowned out the screams of the babies dying in pain.

Sixteen times in as many verses in the Bible, God condemned this practice. In the third book of the Bible, God instructed Moses:

Say to the Israelites: "Any Israelite or any alien

living in Israel who gives any of his children to Molech must be put to death. The people of the community are to stone him." Leviticus 20:2

Twice more in that chapter, God made it clear that parents who murdered their own babies were to be killed.

In listing the sins that caused God to allow Judah to be captured by Babylon, God spoke through the prophet Jeremiah:

They built high places for Baal in the Valley of Ben Hinnom to sacrifice their sons and daughters to Molech, though I never commanded, nor did it enter My mind, that they should do such a detestable thing and so make Judah sin.

Jeremiah 32:35

God had never envisioned His creatures wanting to destroy their creation.

This Valley of Ben Hinnom, where the Israelites sacrificed their children, was also known as Gehenna. Christ used Gehenna as a symbol of Hell itself (see the Greek of Matthew 23:15).

God succinctly said:

Do not give any of your children to be sacrificed to Molech, for you must not profane the name of your God. I am the LORD. Leviticus 18:21

If the Bible were being written today, this verse would probably say "Do not abort any of your children, for you must not profane the name of your God."

ADOPTING THE BABY OUT

If abandonment and abortion are unacceptable options to a Christian, then the man facing fatherhood has only two options left: put the child up for adoption or accept the coming of another life into the family.

There are times when the coming of a baby works unusual hardships on a marriage. Whether these perceived difficulties are valid or not, there is an option of adopting the baby out to live with another couple who will love the child as their own. Although few married couples find themselves in such desperate circumstances that they will offer up their baby for adoption, there are times when this is the best choice for all concerned.

There are thousands of American couples who are unable to conceive a child and who are standing in a long line waiting to adopt a baby. Giving the baby up for adoption meets two needs: it relieves the natural parents of the responsibility of raising a child, and it brings the joy of parenting to an infertile couple.

In America, the courts process over a million adoption cases a year. This means that the joy of life

17

has been extended to more than a million babies who were not terminated in the womb, and that the joy of parenting has been given to a million or more couples. What seemed to be an unbearable burden to one couple became an untold blessing to another.

ACCEPTING PARENTAL RESPONSIBILITIES

The fourth option facing a startled father-to-be is to accept his parental responsibilities. Unless the couple is facing such difficult circumstances that they cannot care for a child and must place the baby with adoptive parents, accepting parental responsibilities is the manly thing to do and is certainly the Christian thing to do.

No man should feel that he is standing alone in facing this challenge, for over four million babies are born annually in our great country. Babies are an industry of their own. Doctors, hospitals, diaper services, clothing manufacturers, food manufacturers, furniture companies, and school systems all depend upon the coming of babies. The world is ready for your baby, and you can get ready too, for God graciously gives parents nine months in which to adapt to their new roles.

Although babies come into the world by the millions, your baby will be far more than a statistic. This child will be a unique individual with the combined qualities of the mother and father, as well as those of the grandparents. The baby comes as a moldable lump of clay ready to respond to your hands. You are about to fashion a life to fit both time and eternity.

Is this a scary thought? Yes! But, again, you are not in this alone. You'll be amazed at the innate wisdom your wife will display in child-raising, and usually you'll receive help from your own families. As we'll discuss later in the section on grandparenting, you will probably find that your parents and your wife's parents are at least as excited about the new baby as you are. The grandparents will contribute much of the wisdom they acquired in raising you and your wife.

You also can expect the help of your church and your church family. If you are not warmly related to a local congregation, start shopping this Sunday. You'll need all the help the church can give you.

In some ways, you and your wife will be on your own, but being a father need not be totally a trial-and-error proposition. Often there are courses available in junior colleges. There are books available at the public library, and several magazines on the newsstands are specifically for parents. Through these you can learn from the experiences of others. Thousands of men before you have handled the responsibility of being a father. Surely you, too, can rise to the occasion.

My Father and I

FATHERHOOD IS GOD'S PLAN

Becoming a father is one of God's major ways of bringing a male into mature manhood. A man's mother will have done her best to make a man out of her son, and his wife may have worked miracles in civilizing him, but the final step in maturity is often through fatherhood. When Dad sees an extension of himself in his baby, it becomes an ultimate challenge to put his personal childhood away and to invest his energies and resources in his child. His focus moves from himself to his newborn infant.

The Bible places the raising of children on a high priority level:

Be fruitful and increase in number; fill the earth and subdue it. Genesis 1:28

Similarly, when Noah and his family were released from the ark after the flood had subsided:

Then God blessed Noah and his sons, saying to them, "Be fruitful and increase in number and fill the earth." Genesis 9:1

God gave us sex for more than physical pleasure and marital unity. He purposed that we reproduce ourselves generation after generation.

Accepting the Role of Father

The mention of fathers more than fifteen hundred times in the Bible gives dads a place of great visibility and responsibility in God's sight. Becoming a father is one of the most Godlike things a man can do, for we share some of God's creative power in our own procreation. We bring into this world a creature very much like ourselves. We also share the responsibility of caring for our creation.

Fatherhood is a participation in the nature of God, for He has revealed Himself as our heavenly Father. Throughout the Bible, we are called His children, and He exercises care and offers provision for us as our Father. It was by God's design that when the disciples asked Jesus to teach them to pray, He said:

> *This, then, is how you should pray: "Our Father in heaven, hallowed be Your name."*
>
> Matthew 6:9

Relationship was placed before request. Jesus implied that God responds to our needs out of responsibility as a Father more than as a benefactor showing pity upon petitioners:

> *So do not worry, saying, "What shall we eat?" or "What shall we drink?" or "What shall we wear?" For the pagans run after all these things, and your heavenly Father knows that you need them.*
>
> Matthew 6:31-32

What a great pattern for modern dads!
In Solomon's psalm, he said:

> *Sons are a heritage from the* Lord, *children a reward from Him. Like arrows in the hands of a warrior are sons born in one's youth. Blessed is the man whose quiver is full of them. They will not be put to shame when they contend with their enemies in the gate.* Psalm 127:3-5

Solomon viewed children as assets, not liabilities. He saw them as protectors of the parents rather than as constant dependents upon them.

While we learn from Solomon that children are an asset, we must remember his other lesson: children are not a biological accident. They are a gift from God our Father. The Bible mentions children over eighteen hundred times in the Old and New Testaments, so they must be special to Father God. When He was here on earth, Jesus took time to bless the children. On at least one occasion, He set a child in the midst of His disciples:

> *And He said: "I tell you the truth, unless you change and become like little children, you will never enter the kingdom of heaven. Therefore, whoever humbles himself like this child is the greatest in the kingdom of heaven. And whoever welcomes a little child like this in My name welcomes Me."* Matthew 18:3-5

Accepting the Role of Father

Jesus saw children as little people and treated them as such.

THE BIBLE'S ADMONITION TO DADS

Since fatherhood is so important to God, we can expect to find some quality instruction in His Book. When Abraham so longed for a son that God opened Sarah's womb at the age of ninety and let her bear the patriarch Isaac, God said the reason He would give Abraham a son was:

> *For I have chosen him, so that he will direct his children and his household after him to keep the way of the LORD by doing what is right and just, so that the LORD will bring about for Abraham what He has promised him.* Genesis 18:19

Is it possible that this is why God has let you bring children into the world, too? Does God see that you will teach your children the ways of the Lord and bring them into the covenants He has established with you?

The Bible speaks of children as being a reward from God, and it even suggests that God is an active agent in the formation of children. God said through the prophet Isaiah:

> *This is what the LORD says—your Redeemer, who formed you in the womb: I am the LORD, who has*

made all things, who alone stretched out the heavens, who spread out the earth by Myself.

Isaiah 44:24

When Jesus spoke of those persons over whom He had responsibility, He said:

My Father, who has given them to Me, is greater than all; no one can snatch them out of My Father's hand. John 10:29

If Jesus could accept these "sheep," as He called them, as a gift from His Father's hand, we should accept our children as His special gift to us. He has called us to become workers together with Him in repopulating the Earth.

The Book of Proverbs says:

Train a child in the way he should go, and when he is old he will not turn from it. Proverbs 22:6

What a privilege! What a responsibility! The shaping of a mature adult is something God entrusts to parents, often when they are very young themselves.

The Bible assumes that children will become like their parents. When they don't, it is the exception and not the rule. Our children will learn more from our example than from our exhortations. They tend to do what we do far more than what we say. As the saying goes, "Your life speaks so loudly, I can't hear what you're saying."

Becoming a parent, then, is far more than a biological process. It is equally a maturing process. We need to exercise the necessary discipline to live the life we want our child to live—to develop life principles we desire to instill in our offspring. We must become, in advance, what we want our child to become.

"Like father, like son" is more than a proverb; it is often a fact of life.

Slowly coming out of the fog of shock, the young man embraces his wife enthusiastically and looking into her questioning eyes, he reassuringly says, "You've made me the happiest man on the face of the Earth. I just hope I can be as good a father as you will be a mother."

"Don't be silly," she says with a girlish giggle. "Before I ever accepted your marriage proposal, I had determined that you would be a good father. If we have a son, I want him to be just like you."

More frequently than not, this is just what happens. Dad becomes the living example of his son's future manhood. Who he is and what he does will influence his son far more than anything he says.

Just as the father becomes the role model for his child, so Dad needs a role model for fatherhood. Where can he find a good one?

TWO

A SEARCH FOR ROLE MODELS

I am telling you what I have seen in the Father's presence, and you do what you have heard from your father. John 8:38

Jesus told the religious leaders of His day, "I am telling you what I have seen in the Father's presence, and you do what you have heard from your father." Jesus ministered to people here on Earth the way He had seen His Father relate to angels in Heaven. Most of us also do what we have seen authority figures in our lives do.

"Monkey see, monkey do" is a cliché based on observation, and of course it is true of people as well as monkeys. We so often do to others what was done to us. We behave like others we have observed in similar situations. For example, children will use their knives and forks in the same manner in which they have observed their parents using them. Personal experiences mold personal behavior.

Similarly, new fathers tend to treat their children as they themselves were treated by their own fathers.

Obviously, then, the first and most important role model for us as fathers is our own earthly father. Good, bad, or indifferent, the way our fathers treated us became our model of fatherhood. As we grew older, we saw other fathers and sometimes recognized weaknesses in our own father by comparison, but he was still our dad.

In situations where the father was a good father, good principles of fatherhood were deeply ingrained in us. We desired to be a father just like our dad. In other cases, our father might have been a failure, and we learned from him how not to be a father. Amazingly, bad examples can be good teachers, too. God taught David the principles of being a king by placing him under the authority of Saul, whom God had rejected as king. By observation, David learned how not to function as a king. Whether as a good example or as an example of failure, our initial role model was our earthly father.

A dinner meeting on a ministry trip furnished me with an example of men learning behavior from their fathers. Pushing back my chair from the table at the restaurant, I told my hosts, "I need to get to bed. I have to get up before breakfast! I leave for the airport at five A.M."

"I always get up before breakfast," my host laughingly teased me. "I don't," his wife said. "From the day we were married until now, my husband brings a cup of coffee to my bedside and places it on a stand.

The pleasing aroma gently wakes me up, and the coffee becomes my breakfast."

I complimented the husband for his thoughtfulness through the years and admitted that this was not part of my daily ritual.

"I thought I was unique in this until two years ago when I mentioned this to my brothers at a family reunion," he told me. "To my amazement, my four brothers confessed that they had done the same thing from day one of their marriages."

"Why do we do this?" my youngest brother asked.

"After a brief discussion, we realized that we had seen our father do it all of our lives. Like father, like son. He was our role model."

THE NEED TO SEARCH

It is unfortunate that not all homes have a father to act as a role model. Not only is it a great negative for the growing children, but it also leaves a great void in their understanding of fatherhood. If boys have never had a father, how can they know how to be a father? After they marry and have children, they have no natural point of reference to guide them. They must look outside their personal experience to find a role for fatherhood.

Thank God for books. Some men learn well from books, while others learn better from instruction.

Readers of the English language have an abundance of books on child-raising. We can also rejoice in the many special conferences and retreats being conducted for men and fathers in our generation. The anointed teaching in these sessions has made a great difference in the lives of many young fathers.

Yet, as valid and valuable as books and conferences are, observation is still the most powerful teaching tool. Seeing another father function properly is the most efficient learning experience a young father can have.

But where are the twentieth-century role models for fathers? We don't find them on television very often. Fathers are frequently ridiculed and pictured as incompetent. Current movies don't usually exemplify quality fatherhood either, nor do today's sports figures. Too frequently even Christian pastors set a poor example of fatherhood for their parishioners.

With so many single-parent homes and such a high divorce rate, we may be hard pressed to find a favorable father image in our neighborhoods.

OLD TESTAMENT FATHER FIGURES

"Go to the Bible for your example," you might say. Go where in the Bible? The first father, Adam, forfeited his divine inheritance through sin. His sons never saw the Garden of Eden. Furthermore, their parental training must have been meager, for the eldest son, Cain, murdered his brother, Abel, over the proper way to worship. Not a very good pattern for us to follow!

Moses is possibly the most revered of the Old Testament fathers. Many Jews call him "the father of Israel," but what kind of father was he? All we know of his fatherhood is that he had children. The Bible simply says:

The sons of Moses: Gershom and Eliezer.

1 Chronicles 23:15

The Bible mentions his sons only once again, in the genealogical records where Gershom's and Eliezer's sons are listed.

Perhaps Moses did not properly develop his sons' potential. Under the tremendous pressure of leading Israel, Moses may have left the rearing of the family to his wife, Zipporah. The Bible never mentions the boys as holding any level of leadership among the Israelites. The Bible doesn't even say that they entered the Promised Land under the leadership of Joshua. It is very possible that they died in the wilderness with their rebellious peers.

Most males are capable of producing children, but not all of them are dedicated enough to become real fathers to their children. Dedication to business often nullifies dedication to family. In trying to provide well for the family, we men frequently substitute money and things for personal attention and training. This may have been the situation with Moses. In any case, the Bible doesn't give us enough detail about Moses' relationship with his sons for us to use him as a role model for fatherhood.

As for Abraham, he wasn't a very good pattern either. God told him:

I have made you a father of many nations.
Genesis 17:5

In his anxiety to help fulfill this promise, Abraham took his wife's maid, Hagar, and had a son (Ishmael) by her. Hagar served as a surrogate mother. Some years later, when God gave Abraham a son through his wife Sarah, Abraham bonded so closely with this promised son, Isaac, that his favoritism made their home an unbearable place for Ishmael and Hagar. Eventually he threw the two of them out, supplying them with only a loaf of bread and a jug of water.

Abraham never outgrew his extreme favoritism for Isaac. Prejudice and favoritism in a father are always disruptive and destructive to a family. The Bible says:

Fathers, do not provoke or irritate or fret your children [do not be hard on them or harass them],

lest they become discouraged and sullen and mo-
rose and feel inferior and frustrated. [Do not break
their spirit].   Colossians 3:21, AMP

So, we'd better rule out Abraham as a favorable role model for fatherhood. He did all of this and more to Ishmael.

"Like father, like son" is a truism, but sometimes a boy will be just like his grandfather. Jacob, like Abraham, fathered children by more than one woman, and the favoritism he displayed toward Joseph (the first son born to him by his beloved Rachel) caused division in the family. Like grandfather, like grandson. Even though Jacob was chosen by God as an instrument through which to build the nation of Israel, surely Jacob's behavior is not intended by God to be a model of fatherhood.

How about King David? He molded the kingdom of Israel through his conquests of surrounding nations and with his strong administrative talents, but what kind of father was he? For the most part, he seems to have been an absentee father. The many wives of David lived together in a harem-like situation. They evidently raised their children in community living, while David occupied the palace. His wives and concubines came and went at David's invitation, but it is likely that the children seldom had access to their father.

David's relationship to his son Absalom betrays

his inability to express his love to his son, although he could talk of it to others. Judging by the way Absalom turned out, David seems to have been an indulgent father who exercised little or no discipline over his children. This is hardly the example modern fathers need to follow.

It is strange how silent the Bible is about the relationship between the godly men of Scripture and their children. Were the prophets good fathers? It would seem that Elijah and Elisha were celibate, so we'll count them out as role models for fathers. Of the minor prophets, only Hosea speaks of having fathered children. He was married to an unfaithful wife and never mentions what he did to provide care for the children during the seasons she was gone from him. Hosea's example doesn't teach us much that is useful as a model of fatherhood beyond his honoring the marriage covenant, even when his wife continued to be a prostitute.

Just as we know little about the family life of the minor prophets (so called because the books they wrote are relatively small), we know insignificantly little about the parental roles of the major prophets. What do we know about the great prophet Isaiah as a father? Almost nothing! We know that he married a prophetess and that God gave him special prophetic names for two of his children, but we are told nothing of Isaiah's relationship to these sons.

At God's instruction, the prophet Jeremiah never

married. In contrast to this, Ezekiel was married, but his wife died fairly early in his prophetic ministry. If they had any children, he never mentioned it in his lengthy book.

After years of reading the Old Testament, I still cannot find a good role model for fathers in its pages.

NEW TESTAMENT FATHER FIGURES

The New Testament tells us less about the personal lives of its main characters than the Old Testament does about its major characters. We know absolutely nothing about the role of the twelve apostles as fathers. If they had children, the Bible never mentions that fact. Since all three of the synoptic Gospels mention Peter's mother-in-law, we know that Peter was married, but whether his wife was alive during the time he ministered with Jesus, we simply don't know. We also don't know whether he fathered any children.

"How about Paul?" you may ask. If you want to get into a quick argument with Bible scholars, raise the subject of whether or not Paul was married. You won't find your answer in anything he wrote, although he did advise single people to remain single so as to better serve the Lord (see 1 Corinthians 7). One thing is certain: Paul made no allusions to having been a father.

Was Dr. Luke a father? He wrote nearly one-third

of the New Testament, but we never hear of his being a father. We don't even know whether he was married. If he was, he was certainly absent from home a great deal of the time, for he traveled with Paul on his missionary journeys.

The personal lives of the authors of Hebrews, James, and Jude are never mentioned in the Bible either. Not one of the writers of the New Testament is identified as a father, much less as a role model of fatherhood.

One of the few model fathers we find in the Gospels is Joseph. God chose him to be the husband of Mary, and the earthly father figure for Jesus. We read of his submission to the will of God, and of his care for Mary and Jesus. In order for Mary to choose him for her husband and for Father God to choose him to raise His Son from infancy, he must have been a holy and righteous man. Yet the information the Bible gives us about him is disappointingly limited.

Some have wondered why Jesus never married and had children. He would have been such a perfect example of a husband and a father, but Jesus didn't come to Earth to be that kind of example. He came to be our Redeemer. He allowed nothing to interfere with His high calling to be the sacrificial lamb for a sinful people. His main role was to release people from the power and penalty of sin and to restore them to a loving relationship with God.

No, the Bible doesn't seem to offer any detailed role models for today's fathers. Perhaps we can chalk this up to the fact that the Bible was written to reveal God's plan of salvation to mankind and the story was edited to its most salient points, leaving the human imagination to fill in many details.

THE LACK OF MODELS BREEDS FRUSTRATION

This lack of examples of good fathers makes it difficult for modern fathers, but it seems that the role of the father has always been difficult. Just as we lack good examples of fatherhood, so did our Bible heroes. No one trained them or us to be dads. We all learn not only by example, but by trial and error, and the firstborn is our pilot model.

Adding to the inexperience we men faced when that first baby was placed in our arms is our insecurity as men. The role of manhood in America is very clouded. As women have expanded and strengthened their roles in life, there has often been a backlash against masculinity. Far too often men don't know what is expected of them in society. Many of us are still confused over our role as husbands, leaving us with no firm emotional foundation from which to step into the role of fatherhood.

Added to this frustration are the increasing demands life imposes on men, which leave a minimum of time for fulfilling the greatest role of our lives: fatherhood. God allows us to share with our wives in bringing into this world a living being who looks and acts very much like we do. Like a shapeless lump of clay, the permanent form this child will take depends upon what we do. With a lifetime responsibility like this, we desperately need a role model after which we can pattern our behavior as fathers.

Fortunately, we have such a role model in Father God. His relationship with His Son, Jesus, is a beautiful pattern of the way we should relate and respond to our children—the complete and perfect example for us to follow.

GOD AS JESUS' FATHER

You heard me say, "I am going away and I am coming back to you." If you loved me, you would be glad that I am going to the Father, for the Father is greater than I.   John 14:28

While at the Mount of Olives, Jesus told His disciples of His impending death, burial, and resurrection. Their response was immediate sorrow, but Jesus told them:

If you loved Me, you would be glad that I am going to the Father, for the Father is greater than I.
                                        John 14:28

To the very end, Jesus declared that God was His Father. It was more than an admission; it was a proud identification. Jesus enjoyed being the Son of God.

The verse that pulsates as the heart of the Bible declares:

*For God so loved the world that He gave His one
and only Son, that whoever believes in Him shall
not perish but have eternal life.*   John 3:16

This not only declares God's abiding love for each
of us, it also demonstrably proclaims that He became
a father. Jesus is the only begotten Son of God. As
such, He has His Father's name and nature. He
shares His Father's inheritance and authorities. He
is so much a part of His Father that He testified:

I and the Father are one.   John 10:30

Jesus was far more than a good man. He was more
than a greatly anointed man of God. Although He
functioned as an exemplary teacher, a compassionate miracle worker, and a generous philanthropist,
He was God in the flesh. He came to redeem men
by becoming a man and dying the death for sin that
we all deserved.

At no time did Jesus cease to be God; rather He
willingly laid aside His divine position to embrace
His role as the Son of God incarnate in human flesh.
We must always be careful lest we confuse what He
did with who He was. As the theologians put it, He
was "very God of very God and very man of very
man."

Even before His conception, Jesus was proclaimed to be the Son of God, for when the angel of

the Lord approached Mary to ask permission to use her as the channel for the birth of Jesus, Gabriel told her:

> *The Holy Spirit will come upon you, and the power of the Most High will overshadow you. So the holy one to be born will be called the Son of God.* Luke 1:35

JESUS WAS DECLARED TO BE THE SON OF GOD

The sonship of Jesus is declared forty-seven times in the New Testament. This testimony was given from the highest authority in all of Heaven and from the lowest authority in Hell. It came from believers and unbelievers alike.

On at least two occasions during His ministry on earth, God announced from Heaven:

> *This is My beloved Son, in whom I am well pleased.* Matthew 3:17, KJV

This was so dramatic that the writers of the Scriptures record this statement seven times. There can be no higher authority than this.

The temptation of Jesus following this first proclamation of His sonship was to doubt God's word. Twice the devil said to Him: *"If You are the Son of God ..."* (Luke 4:3 and 9) and suggested ways Jesus could prove His sonship. But Jesus was so certain of who He was, He didn't need to prove it to Himself, to Satan, or to anyone else.

After the confirmation was given at His baptism that He actually was the Son of God, Jesus publicly acknowledged and proclaimed the fact of His sonship. When the religious rulers cast out of the Temple the blind man whom Jesus had healed, John recorded:

> *Jesus heard that they had thrown him out, and when He found him, He said, "Do you believe in the Son of Man?" "Who is He, Sir?" the man asked. "Tell me so that I may believe in Him." Jesus said, "You have now seen Him; in fact, He is the one speaking with you." Then the man said, "Lord, I believe," and he worshiped Him.*
>
> John 9:35-38

The spirit world unquestionably knew who Jesus was while He was here on the Earth. We read:

> *Moreover, demons came out of many people, shouting, "You are the Son of God!" But He rebuked them and would not allow them to speak, because they knew He was the Christ.* Luke 4:41

Christ's disciples came to realize that Jesus was, indeed, the Son of God. When Philip brought

Nathanael to Jesus after the briefest conversation, we read:

> *Then Nathanael declared, "Rabbi, You are the Son of God; You are the King of Israel."*   John 1:49

Later, after Jesus stilled the raging tempest on the Sea of Galilee, we see:

> *Those who were in the boat worshiped Him, saying, "Truly You are the Son of God."*
> Matthew 14:33

Then, when Jesus questioned His disciples as to who people said He was, He responded to their answers with:

> *"But what about you?...Who do you say I am?" Simon Peter answered, "You are the Christ, the Son of the living God."*   Matthew 16:15-16

So on repeated occasions, the disciples declared that Jesus was the Son of God.

When Jesus talked with Martha after the death of her brother Lazarus, Martha told Jesus:

> *Yes, Lord...I believe that You are the Christ, the Son of God, who was to come into the world.*
> John 11:27

So there were more people than just the disciples who came to recognize that God was the Father of Jesus. Mary, Martha, and others believed, too.

The charge that led to the crucifixion of Jesus was this:

> *We have a law, and according to that law He must*
> *die, because He claimed to be the Son of God.*
>
> John 19:7

We are allowed to listen to the jeers of the people who mocked Christ as He hung on the cross:

> *If Thou be the Son of God, come down from the*
> *cross. Likewise also the chief priests mocking Him,*
> *with the scribes and elders, said, He saved others;*
> *Himself He cannot save. If He be the King of Is-*
> *rael, let Him now come down from the cross, and*
> *we will believe Him. He trusted in God; let Him*
> *deliver Him now, if He will have Him: for He said,*
> *I am the Son of God.* Matthew 27:40-43, KJV

Not everyone involved in the crucifixion of Jesus mocked His claims that He was the Son of God. After the physical phenomena that accompanied Christ's death, one centurion was moved:

> *When the centurion and those with him who were*
> *guarding Jesus saw the earthquake and all that*

had happened, they were terrified, and exclaimed,
"Surely He was the Son of God!"

Matthew 27:54

In Romans, Paul's great doctrinal book, he affirmed that the resurrection of Jesus was God's final attestation that Jesus was His Son. Paul wrote that the Gospel he preached also declared it:

Regarding His Son, who as to His human nature
was a descendant of David, and who through the
Spirit of holiness was declared with power to be
the Son of God by His resurrection from the dead:
Jesus Christ our Lord.   Romans 1:3-4

From the proclamation of His coming until His resurrection from the dead, Jesus was declared to be the Son of God—*"His only begotten Son"* (1 John 4:9, KJV).

Long after the ascension of Jesus, when belief in His sonship induced severe persecution, the disciples risked death to proclaim that Jesus was the Son of God. Their writings constantly affirmed their conviction of this truth, and it became the cornerstone of their faith.

The Apostle John declared Jesus to be *"the only begotten Son of God"* four times. In the prologue to his Gospel, he wrote:

*No man hath seen God at any time; the only be-
gotten Son, which is in the bosom of the Father,
He hath declared Him.* John 1:18, KJV

Two verses after declaring Jesus' sonship in his
classic John 3:16, John affirmed:

*He that believeth on Him is not condemned: but
he that believeth not is condemned already, because he hath not believed in the name of the only
begotten Son of God.* John 3:18, KJV

John was convinced that unwavering faith in
Jesus as the only begotten Son of God was the foundation to salvation.

Much later in his life, in his first epistle to the
churches, John reaffirmed that the coming of the Son
of God into the world was God's greatest demonstration of love. He wrote:

*This is how God showed His love among us: He
sent His one and only Son into the world that we
might live through Him.* 1 John 4:9

The sonship of Jesus is spoken of quite widely in
the epistles of the New Testament. John mentioned
Jesus as the Son of God seven times in his epistles.
Paul referred to it four times in his writings, and
the books of Hebrews and Revelation each mention
it at least once. It was not a sub-theme for any of the

apostles. It was the very heart of their Gospel—their "good news."

THE FATHER SHARED HIS NAME WITH HIS SON

Since Jesus is the Son of God, we should be able to get some guidelines for being a proper father from the way God treated Jesus while He was here on the Earth. For starters, the New Testament shows us at least four things Jehovah, our Father God, shared with Jesus from the moment of His birth:

1. His name
2. His nature
3. His goals
4. His glory

In sharing His name, Father God let Jesus begin life with an excellent reputation. Jesus was the Son of God—the Son of Jehovah, the self-existent One. The character of God had already been established and revealed to the Jews. From the first day Jehovah revealed Himself to Abraham as *"The I AM,"* and continued to communicate His nature by at least seven compound names. These names revealed His covenant relationship with His people. He called Himself:

1. Jehovah-Jireh: "the LORD will provide"—our Provider.

2. Jehovah-Nissi: "the LORD our banner"—our Defense.

3. Jehovah-Rapha: "the LORD our physician"—our Healer.

4. Jehovah-Rohi: "the LORD our shepherd"—our Guide.

5. Jehovah-M'kaddesh: "the LORD our holiness"—our Right Standing before God.

6. Jehovah-Tsidkenu: "the LORD our righteousness"—our Right Standing before men.

7. Jehovah-Shammah: "the LORD is present"—our Ever Present One.

Jesus did not have to live down a bad family name. He inherited a great name. It came with His birth. It was His divine heritage. His Father shared it with Him.

Happy is the child who is born to a good name. A good reputation in life, a name for honesty, integrity and morality is a great gift to hand on to your children. People will often judge your children based on their opinion of you. We may not have wealth to share with our children, but the Bible declares:

A good name is more desirable than great riches; to be esteemed is better than silver or gold.
Proverbs 22:1

A good name is better than fine perfume.
Ecclesiastes 7:1

After children have matured, they can establish their own names and reputations, but while they are living at home, they live under the reputation of their parents. What reputation have we given to our children?

THE FATHER SHARED HIS NATURE WITH HIS SON

In sharing His nature with His Son, God assured all whose lives were touched by Jesus that what God is, the Son is. The mercy, grace, faithfulness, and goodness of the God of the Old Testament are resident in the very nature of Jesus in the New Testament.

In looking forward to the coming of Christ, the Old Testament prophet Isaiah had said:

> *For to us a child is born, to us a son is given, and the government will be on His shoulders. And He will be called Wonderful Counselor, Mighty God, Everlasting Father, Prince of Peace.* Isaiah 9:6

What a marvelous description of the nature of Jesus!

Wonderful:

> *But when the chief priests and the teachers of the law saw the wonderful things He did and the children shouting in the temple area, "Hosanna to the Son of David," they were indignant.*
> Matthew 21:15

Counselor: The officers who were sent to arrest Jesus returned to the chief priests and Pharisees without Him and explained their failure with the simple statement:

Never man spake like this man.   John 7:46, KJV

Talk about a counselor!
Mighty God: People in the Temple asked:

From whence hath this man these things? and what wisdom is this which is given unto Him, that even such mighty works are wrought by His hands?   Mark 6:2, KJV

Ten times the things Jesus did were declared to be *"mighty works."*

Everlasting Father: He imparted everlasting life to believers, and Peter spoke of *"the everlasting kingdom of Christ"*:

For so an entrance will be ministered to you abundantly into the everlasting kingdom of our Lord and Savior Jesus Christ.   2 Peter 1:11, KJV

Prince of Peace: Before His ascension, Jesus said:

Peace I leave with you; My peace I give you. I do not give to you as the world gives. Do not let your hearts be troubled and do not be afraid.
                                                   John 14:27

God as Jesus' Father

God is defined as being love, light, holy, and a consuming fire in the New Testament. All of this is consistently seen in the precious Son of God. Jesus consistently demonstrated the nature of His Father.

Children display the nature of their fathers because through their genes fathers pass on that nature to their children. What we are affects our children long before they begin to mimic what we do. A father marks his children with the stamp of his own nature.

GOD SHARED HIS GOALS WITH HIS SON

There has never been such a father-son partnership as was seen between Jesus and His Father. The ultimate purpose of Jesus' coming was established before the world was created. Jesus was *"the Lamb that was slain from the creation of the world"* (Revelation 13:8). Peter emphasized this when he wrote:

> *Forasmuch as ye know that ye were not redeemed with corruptible things, as silver and gold, from your vain conversation received by tradition from your fathers; but with the precious blood of Christ, as of a lamb without blemish and without spot: who verily was foreordained before the foundation of the world, but was manifest in these last times for you.* 1 Peter 1:18-20, KJV

It became obvious that Father and Son shared the

same goal of redemption even before they created Adam and Eve. Throughout His entire ministry, Jesus never allowed anything to deter Him from achieving this goal. He sidestepped popular acclaim, and refused to allow the multitude to make Him king in Jerusalem. He testified:

> *And He that sent me is with me: the Father hath not left me alone; for I do always those things that please him.* John 8:29, KJV

As Jesus entered into His ministry, the Father shared His goals with His Son. They loved the world together, and they worked toward its redemption as a team. When the Jews asked Jesus to plainly tell them whether He was the Christ, He answered them:

> *Do not believe Me unless I do what My Father does.* John 10:37

There is no better way to train a child than to hitch him to his father. Doing things together is even more important than merely being together.

In earlier times in our American culture, sons usually learned their father's trade and joined him in the family business while daughters married and became mothers. This is still a common practice in many cultures around the world. Although Americans today emphasize each individual's right to choose a trade or profession, this doesn't relieve the father of his responsibility to help his children obtain the necessary education and training for their future. If a child doesn't choose to share his father's business or profession, the father can begin to share his children's goals and help make their dreams into realities.

THE FATHER SHARED HIS GLORY WITH HIS SON

In addition to sharing His name, nature, and goals, God also shared His glory with Jesus. Father God highly exalted Jesus. He bragged about Him. At the beginning of Christ's ministry, God publicly declared:

> *This is My Son, whom I love; with Him I am well pleased.* Matthew 3:17

After the close of Jesus' public ministry, we read:

> *Therefore God exalted Him to the highest place and gave Him the name that is above every name.* Philippians 2:9

Praise from a father is a prerequisite for developing a good self-image. Children should hear more than correction from their fathers. They need to hear much commendation. As a matter of principle, parents have no right to punish their children if they have not learned to praise their children.

The glory of the father can be shared with his children. Let them enter into the joy of Dad's achievements. Let them share in a raise, or in a celebration of a promotion.

Does the role of a father seem too difficult and the role models too lacking? Then why did God make it so easy for us to become fathers? Maybe we need to remember His promise:

> *I will instruct you and teach you in the way you should go; I will counsel you and watch over you.*
> Psalm 32:8

Where we lack good earthly models for parenting we can look to God, the original Parent, and learn from Him how to be a quality father in these confused times. After all, He was not only the Father of Jesus, He has become our Father as well.

GOD AS OUR FATHER

Jesus said, "Do not hold on to me, for I have not yet returned to the Father. Go instead to my brothers and tell them, 'I am returning to my Father and your Father, to my God and your God.'"

John 20:17

Jesus was a master at speaking words of comfort. After His ascension, He told Mary Magdalene:

Do not hold on to Me, for I have not yet returned to the Father. Go instead to My brothers and tell them, "I am returning to My Father and your Father, to My God and your God."   John 20:17

What an enforcement to her faith, and to ours as well, to have Jesus declare that His Father is also our Father!

I've already stated that the most obvious role model any man will have for fatherhood is his own father. From infancy into maturity, the day-to-day relationship of a son with his father forms an indelible impression of the parental role of dad. Where dad has been a good father, the impression is a healthy one, and it is likely that the son will also be a good father.

Unfortunately, some fathers are poor or bad examples of fatherhood. They may be absent, uncaring, selfish, poor providers, or even harsh and mean. We are discovering more and more that some fathers are sexual abusers of their children, and that, in turn, these children often become abusers of their own children. Patterns learned in childhood tend to follow us into adulthood. The Bible says:

Train a child in the way he should go, and when he is old he will not turn from it. Proverbs 22:6

The principle is that early training lasts a lifetime. Both good and bad training follow a child into the mature years.

In American society, more and more boys are being raised by their mothers in a single-parent family. These sons have an absentee father or have never even met their father. With little or no male influence in the home, it is difficult for such boys to enter marriage and successfully step into the role of being a father (or even a husband). The lack of a father figure has left them unprepared to be husbands and fathers themselves.

By the time these men have married, it is impossible for them to go back and choose a surrogate father to learn from, but their cause is not hopeless. The human soul is not only capable of learning, it is equally capable of unlearning.

In my early teen years, I earned a portable typewriter by agreeing to do a year of Sunday church bulletins that had preprinted advertising on the fourth page. Having received no instruction in typing, I used the "Columbus system": I just discovered a Key and then landed on it. It was a two-finger operation. I became quite proficient at this, but when I entered high school and signed up for a typing class, I found that what I had taught myself was worse than useless; it was a severe impediment. I had to unlearn before I could learn. It was painful and slow, but I forced myself to learn the touch system of typing.

Similarly, young men can, if necessary, unlearn what their fathers taught them about being a father. They can become students of the art of fatherhood. They can learn from others, from classes, from books, and from interaction with other fathers, and even from their own children. No matter how abused they may have been in their childhood, they need not pass that abuse on to their own children. After all, we can learn good things from a bad example. We can remind ourselves that the way our father related or failed to relate to us is the way not to relate to our family.

My Father and I

The Christian Life Is a New Beginning

There is no place outside of Christ where a person can truly start life over, with the past wiped clean. We may move to a new location, change marriage partners, or try new careers, but our true inner self goes with us into all new endeavors. We are not only unable to forget our past, but there is nothing in our present that we can do to change it. The past is like indelible ink on a white shirt: we have to live with it or replace the shirt.

The peculiarity of the grace of the Gospel is that it gives us a new beginning. Read the gospel accounts of people whose lives were totally turned around by the intervention of Jesus. Listen to today's testimonies of drug addicts who have been saved and restored to a normal life. Look at pastors, elders, and deacons who once lived debased lives, but who now are models of God's grace. The work of the cross of Jesus Christ lets us start over.

Does this seem too theological and impractical to you? Please remember that Jesus didn't come to give us only a Christian religion, a system of beliefs. He came to give us life. He testified:

> *I have come that they may have life, and have it to the full.*   John 10:10

Entering this new life of God is not accomplished

by education, training, or discipline. We are born into it. When Nicodemus, one of the Pharisees, a ruler of the Jews, came to Jesus by night to inquire about spiritual things, the Scriptures record:

> *In reply Jesus declared, "I tell you the truth, no one can see the kingdom of God unless he is born again."* John 3:3

This was too much for Nicodemus:

> *"How can a man be born when he is old?" Nicodemus asked. "Surely he cannot enter a second time into his mother's womb to be born!" Jesus answered, "I tell you the truth, no one can enter the kingdom of God unless he is born of water and the Spirit. Flesh gives birth to flesh, but the Spirit gives birth to spirit."* John 3:4-6

Many years later, Peter wrote:

> *For you have been born again, not of perishable seed, but of imperishable, through the living and enduring word of God.* 1 Peter 1:23

Being born again is not mere preacher talk. It is a provision of God for all who accept Jesus Christ as their Savior. It is our opportunity to start life over. It is God's way of giving us a new beginning. We are not remodeled; we are made new. God doesn't try to repair our life; He replaces it!

The new believer does not add Christ to his life. Quite the contrary, he surrenders his old life to death and burial with Christ, and Jesus becomes a new life in that person. The Bible says:

We were therefore buried with Him through baptism into death in order that, just as Christ was raised from the dead through the glory of the Father, we too may live a new life.   Romans 6:4

Paul, out of personal experience, testified:

Therefore, if anyone is in Christ, he is a new creation; the old has gone, the new has come!
            2 Corinthians 5:17

This means that none of us needs to live with limitations that were imposed upon us as children. Whatever our earthly fathers may have done to us was part of the life that was buried with Jesus at baptism. We are living a new life. We have started over as a new creation. God pushed the delete button at our salvation and gave us a blank screen upon which to write.

Christian fathers have a marvelous resource available to them. Whether or not your past has qualified you to be a dad, your new life in Christ Jesus qualifies you. You have access to the wisdom of God through the operation of the Holy Spirit, the third Person of the Godhead, who takes residence in our lives at our conversion.

Two of the functioning gifts of God's Spirit are the word of wisdom and the word of knowledge (see 1 Corinthians 12:8). God, somewhat like the on-line help in a computer program, dwells in our spirit by the Holy Spirit. He is available on demand. David reminds us:

> *God is our refuge and strength, an ever-present help in trouble.*   Psalm 46:1

James admonished us based on years of experience:

> *If any of you lacks wisdom, he should ask God, who gives generously to all without finding fault, and it will be given to him.*   James. 1:5

GOD IS OUR FATHER

The New Testament not only continuously proclaims that God is the Father of Jesus, it also announces that believers, too, become sons of God. John declared it succinctly when he wrote:

> *Dear friends, now we are children of God, and*

*what we will be has not yet been made known.
But we know that when He appears, we shall be
like Him, for we shall see Him as He is.*

1 John 3:2

No Christian father has the right to hide behind
the argument, "I can't help myself. I'm just like my
father." The Bible tells us:

*Therefore come out from them and be separate,
says the Lord. Touch no unclean thing, and I will
receive you. I will be a Father to you, and you
will be My sons and daughters, says the Lord Almighty.*   2 Corinthians 6:17-18

God, the Father of our Lord Jesus Christ, offers to
become the Father of believers, embracing them as
sons and daughters.

He is not merely our Father according to the law
He has established; He is our practical, live-in Father. It must have been a tremendous shock to the
disciples of Jesus, who were steeped in the Old Testament concept of God as "The Omnipotent One"
and "The Creator of the Earth," to have Jesus teach
them:

*This, then, is how you should pray "Our Father
in heaven, hallowed be Your name."*

Matthew 6:9

It would have been easier for them to begin their prayer with this:

For Thou, LORD, art high above all the earth: Thou art exalted far above all gods.

Psalm 97:9, KJV

But Jesus introduced them to a far more intimate approach to God.

Jesus told us to call God "Father"; in the Gospel it is rendered as the Greek word *pater*, which is a very familiar word for "the male parent." Its equivalent in the English language is "papa" or "daddy."

Jesus was not only teaching them that prayer is communication that flows out of relationship more than it is requests that flow out of perceived needs; He was also emphasizing to them the availability of God as a concerned and loving parent. "Think of God as Daddy," Jesus was saying. He is not only the Father, He is our Father.

The Apostle Paul quickly grasped this concept of God's being his personal Father after his conversion on the road to Damascus. In his writings, Paul spoke of God as *"our Father"* nine times. His standard greeting in his Epistles was:

Grace to you and peace from God our Father, and the Lord Jesus Christ.   Romans 1:7, KJV

He used this greeting or a variant of it in his letters to the churches in Corinth, Galatia, Ephesus, Philippi, Colossae, and Thessalonica. He also used it in his private letter to his friend Philemon. James also spoke of *"God our Father"* (James 1:27).

How wonderful that we receive not only a new life but also a new Father in our conversion. Just as the limitations of our old life were set aside at our baptism, so the limitations of our earthly father's relationship with us are replaced by our new relationship with our heavenly Father. God, not our earthly dad, becomes our primary role model for fatherhood. We learn to look into the Word of God for principles of parenting, rather than just search our memory circuits for guidance.

SINCE GOD IS OUR FATHER, WE SHOULD HAVE HIS NATURE

If God is our Father, and the Bible declares that He is, then His character should be seen in us more than the character of our earthly fathers. His life is in us, we have been born again by His Spirit and His Word, and He has declared that we are His sons and daughters. So something of the nature of God should be seen in our lives. I do not project that Christians are miniature gods—far from it. I have lived far too long to pretend that! As a matter of fact, few attitudes will more quickly disqualify us from being good fathers than an adoption of a "messiah complex." We need to remain approachable people, with all our flaws.

However, to the extent that we learn to surrender control of our lives to the indwelling Holy Spirit, we take on some of the nature and character of God. Some of these qualities of God are called "the fruit of the Spirit." Paul wrote:

> *But the fruit of the Spirit is love, joy, peace, longsuffering, gentleness, goodness, faith, meekness, temperance: against such there is no law.*
> Galatians 5:22-23, KJV

These qualities of God come to us when we receive His Holy Spirit, and they ripen or mature progressively in us as we learn to allow them to replace the works of our flesh on a day-to-day basis. What could better qualify any man to be a father than to be endowed with and controlled by these qualities?

LOVE IS AVAILABLE TO DADS

God's essential nature is love. John repeatedly told us, *"God is love"* (1 John 4:8 and 16). None of us would doubt that God loves, but the Bible declares that God *is* love. When the word love is connected with God, it is in its noun form, not its verb form.

Love is not something that God does; it is something that God *is*. Love is part of His basic nature, and He shares that nature with His sons and daughters.

Since God lives within the believer through His Holy Spirit, we should expect His love to begin to demonstrate itself in our lives. It is the first fruit of the Spirit to ripen in the believer. What an asset this is for fathers, especially young fathers!

The greatest gift any father can give to his children is that he love their mother. Most of us men come into marriage quite dominated by self-love. We are the center of our world, and we are often quite childish about it. Even courtship revolves around us. We tend to focus on our feelings and our needs. The early times in a marriage are often a struggle between our own interests and the greater interests of the marriage team.

The man who refuses to mature emotionally isn't ready for children, for when a child comes into the home, the world revolves around him or her. The essence of love is to center our affections around someone other than ourselves. In his great chapter on love, Paul confessed:

> *When I was a child, I talked like a child, I thought like a child, I reasoned like a child. When I became a man, I put childish ways behind me.*
>
> 1 Corinthians 13:11

God as Our Father

Each of us men needs to follow his example. We need to reach outside ourselves to find an object to love.

JOY IS AVAILABLE TO DADS

The second fruit of the Spirit to display itself in the believer is God's basic nature of joy—not happiness, joy! Our happiness is a result of happenings, but our joy is a response to Jesus. Happenings vary and our happiness vacillates, but Jesus is constant and so is the believer's joy.

A joyful father is a blessing in the life of a child. Pressures of life, anxieties about the future, and the responsibilities of parenthood can squeeze the joy out of life, but we have the assurance:

The joy of the LORD is your strength.
                                        Nehemiah 8:10

If we will allow this second fruit of the Spirit to ripen in our lives, we can face today with a hug and tomorrow with a smile.

PEACE IS AVAILABLE TO DADS

Peace is the essential nature of God. He is called *"the God of peace"* five times in the New Testament. Paul gave this benediction:

*And the peace of God, which transcends all un-
derstanding, will guard your hearts and your
minds in Christ Jesus.*   Philippians 4:7

He pled with us believers:

*And let the peace of God rule in your hearts, to
the which also ye are called in one body; and be ye
thankful.*   Colossians 3:15, KJV

It is terrible when the home becomes a war zone.
It is damaging to our children to see Mom and Dad
engaged in conflict with one another. It greatly
threatens their security. They don't know how to
handle seeing their parents' emotions out of control.
But our emotions need not get out of control, for we
have God dwelling in our lives, and He is a peace-
ful God who gives us peace.

Children are a heavy responsibility and they can,
and will, get on our nerves. At times, they threaten
our authority, and we sometimes "lose our cool" and
react in anger. At those times, we need to take a deep
breath, silently ask the Holy Spirit to help us, and
allow His peace to rule our emotions. We need to
memorize and frequently rehearse this biblical saying:

*A gentle answer turns away wrath, but a harsh
word stirs up anger.*   Proverbs 15:1

LONGSUFFERING IS AVAILABLE TO DADS

The first three fruits of the Spirit reflect our relationship with God, but the next three concern our relationships with others. Few of us have these character traits inherently, but we can receive them from the Holy Spirit, who dwells in us. He not only suffers long with us, but He also enables us to suffer long with others—even our children. How often, in our frustration, have we yelled at one of our children, "Why don't you grow up?" Intellectually we know that maturity is progressive and takes time, but the delay often taxes our inner being. That's when the Holy Spirit grants us the grace to continue to suffer with their immaturity and selfishness. We simply have to learn to look inward for more ability to suffer long. God has suffered a long time with our immaturity, so surely He can give us grace to suffer a little longer with our children's immaturity.

The New International Version of the Bible uses the word "patience" for longsuffering. God shares His immense patience with us. What a gift for fathers! Wise King Solomon wrote:

Patience is better than pride.   Ecclesiastes 7:8

The apostle Paul admonished us:

Be patient with everyone. 1 Thessalonians 5:14

That certainly includes our children.

We have been told for generations that patience is a virtue. We learn it through the Christian life. Paul told us:

We glory in tribulations also: knowing that tribulation worketh patience. Romans 5:3, KJV

James wrote:

The trying of your faith worketh patience.
James 1:3, KJV

But I'm glad to tell you that times of testing and tribulation are not the only things that produce patience. Patience is a fruit of the Spirit. God's patience dwells in our lives, and we can nurture that fruit and be patient ourselves. Our Father is patient and He shares His nature with us.

GENTLENESS IS AVAILABLE TO DADS

Gentleness is also a part of God's inherent nature. The Bible speaks of Him as our Shepherd—one who tenderly cares for all our wants and needs. He doesn't scatter; He gathers. He doesn't drive; He leads. His gentleness in all His dealings with us induces a comfortable trust.

He makes this same gentleness available to believers through the resident fruit of the Spirit.

Children need to see gentleness in their fathers. Even if their dad is gruff by nature, the grace of God can give him a very gentle nature in the home. Gentleness is strength; not weakness. Any man can bully his way around, but a truly strong man who is in control of his life can be gentle in his dealings in the home.

Nothing can draw the gentle nature out of a man faster than having his baby placed in his arms. When he looks at the helpless infant, emotions rise to the surface—emotions the father didn't know he possessed—and he is overwhelmed by them. It is not unusual, nor is it unmanly, to see a new father gently weep as he looks at his son or daughter cuddled in his arms.

When we look at King David, we are tempted to see his greatness in his military conquests, but he said to God:

> *Thy gentleness hath made me great.*
> Psalm 18:35, KJV

There is strength in gentleness. Gentle kindness is a beautiful attribute for a father, but not all men have this disposition naturally. As Christians, however, we have access to this gentle kindness in the Holy Spirit, who dwells in our spirits. God is gentle and kind in His dealings with us, and He will help us fathers to be kind to our wives and children if we will simply ask Him.

GOODNESS IS AVAILABLE TO DADS

Are any believers unaware that God is a good God? The Bible declares it, defines it, and consistently demonstrates it. David exclaimed:

How great is Your goodness, which You have stored up for those who fear You, which You bestow in the sight of men on those who take refuge in You.   Psalm 31:19

Most Christian men deeply desire to be good men, but we know that our human nature is selfish and bent toward evil. We may learn to conform to the rules of society and to the laws of God, and we may look good, but we know our hearts. We need a source of inward goodness that is beyond our ability to produce, and the Holy Spirit is God's source of divine goodness to us men.

David seemed to be well aware of the gift of God's goodness, for he wrote:

Surely goodness and mercy shall follow me all the days of my life: and I will dwell in the house of the LORD for ever.   Psalm 23:6, KJV

If God's goodness pursues us, perhaps we should slow down from time to time and let it catch up to us.

It is interesting that David connected the presence of God's goodness with dwelling continually in the house of the Lord. The more time we spend in His divine presence, the greater the measure of God's goodness that will be seen in our lives. When our minds are centered on the Lord Jesus, His goodness to us flows out as a great goodness through us. Godly men are good men. It is a gift of the Spirit in their hearts and lives.

America desperately needs good men in her homes. The Church will be strengthened if more good men will take roles of leadership, and our nation longs to have good men holding office, but this goodness must come out of a personal relationship with God. As we dwell in His presence, His goodness overwhelms our selfish natures. The fruit of goodness is in every Christian father. He merely needs to pick the fruit and partake of it. Paul assured us:

For the fruit of the Spirit is in all goodness and righteousness and truth.   Ephesians 5:9, KJV

FAITHFULNESS IS AVAILABLE TO DADS

Although the King James Version of the Bible calls the seventh fruit of the Spirit *"faith,"* almost all other English translations use the word *"faithfulness."* In his letter to the church at Rome, Paul said:

So then faith cometh by hearing, and hearing by the word of God.   Romans 10:17, KJV

Faith, then, is a result of hearing the Gospel; faithfulness is a fruit of the Spirit.

Early in God's revelation of Himself to the children of Israel after they came out of Egypt, He told them:

> *Know therefore that the LORD your God is God; He is the faithful God, keeping His covenant of love to a thousand generations of those who love Him and keep His commands.*
>
> Deuteronomy 7:9

God makes His faithfulness available to us.

Happy is the home that has a faithful father. The man who is sexually faithful to his wife brings a great stability to the family. When he is a faithful provider, the physical needs of the home are consistently answered. When he is a faithful lover of his children, their emotional needs are satisfied. When he is a faithful worshiper of God, the spiritual needs of the children will be fulfilled.

Commitment is almost a foreign word to our American society, but it is a Bible concept that is so necessary that the Holy Spirit blossoms, buds, and bears the fruit of faithfulness in the lives of believers. When temptation to unfaithfulness begins to overwhelm a father, he should immediately go to God in prayer and ask for this fruit of the Spirit to ripen in his life.

Meekness Is Available to Dads

Meekness, as the word is used in the Bible, should never be equated with weakness. Meekness means humility or teachableness. We look at Moses as an example of strength and manhood (and he was), but God said of this great father of Israel:

Now the man Moses was very meek, above all the men which were upon the face of the earth.
Numbers 12:3, KJV

The New International Version translates this verse:

Now Moses was a very humble man, more humble than anyone else on the face of the earth.

Jesus said of Himself:

Take my yoke upon you, and learn of me; for I am meek and lowly in heart: and ye shall find rest unto your souls. Matthew 11:29, KJV

If He, the Son of God, was meek (*"gentle and humble in heart,"* NIV), then this same grace of God must be available to fathers in the home.

The promises God gives to the meek are glorious:

The meek shall eat and be satisfied: they shall praise the LORD *that seek Him: your heart shall live for ever.*   Psalm 22:26, KJV

The meek will He guide in judgment: and the meek will He teach His way.   Psalm 25:9, KJV

The meek shall inherit the earth; and shall delight themselves in the abundance of peace.
       Psalm 37:11, KJV

The LORD *lifteth up the meek: He casteth the wicked down to the ground.*   Psalm 147:6, KJV

The Bible abounds with many other promises given to the meek—those who are humble of heart and open to instruction. What a comfort this should be to young fathers who think they are supposed to know everything about their role in life, when they actually are terrified by how very little they know! The indwelling Holy Spirit will give a meek and teachable spirit to the man who asks for it.

TEMPERANCE IS AVAILABLE TO DADS

The New International Version of the Bible uses the word "self-control," which is the true meaning of the Greek word for "temperance" used in Galatians 5:23. God wants us to control our emotions rather than be controlled by them. He has given us strong passions, but He intends for us to master them, not for us to be enslaved by them. Wise King Solomon said:

He that is slow to anger is better than the mighty; and he that ruleth his spirit than he that taketh a city. Proverbs 16:32, KJV

As every man knows, this is easier said than done!

There are few places in a man's life where temperance or self-control is more important than in his home. His relationships with his wife, sons, and daughters demand tremendous self-control. If he gets out of control, the entire home will be out of control. Many modern males have had little control exerted over their lives. They have run the streets and have done anything they pleased. This won't work in the home. The family unit demands temperance and self-control. If men didn't learn self-control in their homes as youth, then where are they, as fathers-to-be, going to get it? The Holy Spirit provides it in the believer's spirit. When the believer yields control of his life to the indwelling Holy Spirit, he finds the ability to control himself in all situations. This qualifies him to be a leader of his family.

Beautifully, God does not require from us anything He has not offered to us. As Peter told the lame man at Gate Beautiful:

Such as I have give I thee.   Acts 3:6, KJV

We have a measure of the nature of God dwelling within us in the fruit of the Spirit. Let's pass it on to our children. All of these graces are inherent in the nature of God, and He is our Father. He is happy to pass on to us what we lack so we can have a full life and be quality fathers of our children.

As our Father, God has not only shared His nature with us, but He also has become our prime example of fatherhood in the way He related to His only begotten Son, Jesus.

FIVE

BONDING WITH YOUR CHILD

I and the Father are one.   John 10:30

It is such a simple statement that we are in danger of missing its importance. *"I and My Father are one."* What union! What communion! What bonding! Wouldn't it be wonderful if you and your child could bond so completely?

During the final years of David's hiding from King Saul, he lived in the Philistine city of Ziklag. From time to time others who were in Saul's disfavor came to David, seeking to join forces with him. On one of these occasions, men from the tribes of Benjamin and Judah approached David's camp:

> *And David went out to meet them, and answered and said unto them, If ye be come peaceably unto me to help me, mine heart shall be knit unto you.*
> 1 Chronicles 12:17, KJV

The New International Version of the Bible translates that final phrase, *"I am ready to have you unite with me."*

This is what is meant by bonding. It is the knitting or uniting of two persons. Bonding between mother and child is almost an automatic process. As the baby grows in the mother's womb, the two of them are physically linked or knit together. The baby's life depends on this link. Through the months of gestation, mother and child form a strong emotional bond, so that by the delivery date, the two of them are united as a team. The baby instinctively knows the mother.

This bonding does not automatically occur with fathers. Quite frequently Dad distances himself from the pregnancy and birth. His contribution to the coming of a child was brief and pleasurable, but he may have disregarded it when it was over. Often the husband resents his wife's pregnancy, and deliberately distances himself from it. He frequently builds an emotional wall between himself and his wife at a time when she needs his support and acceptance the most.

This is seldom a conscious act of cruelty on the part of the husband. It is more likely an ignorant response to a new circumstance. His body isn't undergoing the physical, chemical, and emotional changes his wife is experiencing. She will be conscious of her pregnancy every waking moment of her life for the next nine months, but this same great event will be far in the back of Dad's mind most of the time.

Bonding With Your Child

The husband will not experience morning sickness or nights of sleeplessness. He will not know what it is like to be awakened in the night with a restless baby kicking and turning inside him. He will have difficulty understanding the emotional mood swings in his wife. He may resent the loss of his wife's girl-like figure and the enforced sexual limitations placed on him.

Many men resent the coming of a baby into their homes and dislike the changes a baby will bring. Initially he may see only competition for his wife's attention and affection. Although he is glad that it's not another man who has captured his wife's affection, he realizes that this little person has won her heart even before being born into the world. He views the baby as a competitor, and senses that he will seldom win in this competition.

Bonding During the Prenatal Period

The best answer to this needless conflict is for you, the husband, to learn to bond with your child much as the mother has. Bringing a child into the world should be a team effort. It is a process to be shared by you and your wife. It is possible for you to become emotionally involved in this pregnancy from its early beginning so that you and your child will be bonded, or knit together, even before you know whether you will have a son or a daughter.

It seems obvious that God the Father bonded with Jesus His Son before Jesus was even born. Before Jesus was conceived, Father God sent His angel Gabriel to discuss this possibility with Mary. Gabriel told her:

> *He will be great and will be called the Son of the Most High. The Lord God will give Him the throne of His father David.*   **Luke 1:32**

After Mary agreed to bear God's Son, Father again dispatched Gabriel, but this time He sent him to Joseph, who was engaged to marry this teenaged girl.

An angel of the Lord appeared to him in a dream and said:

> *Joseph son of David, do not be afraid to take Mary home as your wife, because what is conceived in her is from the Holy Spirit. She will give birth to a Son, and you are to give Him the name Jesus, because He will save His people from their sins.*
> **Matthew 1:20-21**

Like the dad who purchases a football for his unborn son, Father God was bragging about His Son and foretelling what Jesus would do. Perhaps this is a good role model for us to follow. Talk with your wife about your coming baby. Begin to build dreams for your child (recognizing that your child may pursue different dreams, and that this is not wrong).

Plan together for this addition to your family. Work together in preparing a place for the baby. Can you fix up a nursery, or will you put a crib in the corner of your bedroom? Share with your wife in securing the necessary baby furniture. Although you won't be invited to the baby shower, your wife can tell you the details while she shows you the gifts. Make yourself become interested. It will not only enhance your wife's pleasure, it also will help bond you to your coming child.

Beyond merely talking with your wife about the coming baby, you would help yourself, and perhaps the baby, by talking to the unborn infant—especially in the final two months of the pregnancy. It will force you to think of the baby as a person, and it gives the baby a chance to get to know your voice before ever seeing you. This can create an invisible bond between you and your child. Father God did this to His Son before He was born. When Mary was a few months pregnant, she went to visit her cousin Elizabeth:

> *When Elizabeth heard Mary's greeting, the baby leaped in her womb, and Elizabeth was filled with the Holy Spirit. In a loud voice she exclaimed: Blessed are you among women, and blessed is the child you will bear! But why am I so favored, that the mother of my Lord should come to me? As*

soon as the sound of your greeting reached my ears, the baby in my womb leaped for joy. Blessed is she who has believed that what the Lord has said to her will be accomplished! Luke 1:41-45

Even before the Day of Pentecost, God filled Elizabeth with the Holy Spirit so that He could speak approvingly to His Son in Mary's womb.

You may not believe that the unborn child could recognize your voice, but he can. Talk to your growing baby in the womb. If Father God talked to His Son while the boy was still in the womb, why shouldn't you talk to your unborn child? Of course the infant won't understand a word you say, but your baby will make an identification with your voice. The developing baby can also identify with your moods. Gentleness, calmness, and love expressed in the home will give the coming child a sense of security.

Touch forms a quick bond between persons. Sometimes, when our first baby was kicking in my wife's womb, my wife would take my hand, place it on her protruding belly, and say, "Feel that? Your baby's responding to your voice." Whether or not this was true, it produced a high level of emotion in me. I was sharing in sensations my wife had previously experienced alone.

The more prenatal experiences you can share with your wife, the greater the bond will be between you and your coming child. Don't let her have this child all alone. It is your production, too, you know. Share in the emotions. Participate in the mystery of bringing another human into this world. Begin the bonding process early in the pregnancy.

BONDING DURING THE BIRTH PROCESS

In the days when my children were born, it was almost unheard of for a husband to be in the delivery room with his wife. I stood by my wife while the contractions were becoming more frequent, but when she was wheeled into the delivery room, I was shunted into a waiting room. Still, I had shared in the birthing process.

Today it is quite common for the husband to be allowed to view and emotionally participate in the delivery. What a privilege it is to share with your wife in this miracle of life!

God shared in the birth of Jesus. I wonder if Mary ever experienced the presence of God more fully than while she was giving birth to Jesus. Father God sent angels to announce in the heavens that His Son was born. He urged humble shepherds to come to the manger, and He guided the wise men from the East to come and worship Jesus.

Not being there during the birth of your child (unless you can't possibly avoid being away) is unfair to the mother, to the child, and to yourself. A wonderful time of bonding is lost when the father is denied participation in the birth, for whatever reason. I'll never forget the overwhelming sense of awe that flowed over me when the nurse showed me my first baby. I'm certain that I said all sorts of foolish things, for words are such inefficient tools for expressing deep emotion, but the feeling of pride that welled up in me engulfed me in joy.

I was a father! That was my daughter! I was a man! My spirit soared in thanksgiving to God, and I couldn't wait to hug my wife and tell her how very proud I was of her for helping me reproduce myself.

Yes, my nature was reproduced in my children, even though they were all girls.

BONDING DURING INFANT CARE

Father God did not abandon Mary after Jesus was born. He bonded with Jesus in Christ's infancy. When Mary took Jesus to the Temple for His dedication, God spoke to Mary and the infant Jesus through the prophet Simeon and the prophetess Anna. It was God's way of participating in this act of dedication.

To some, it may seem effeminate for the father to help with the care of the infant, but to do so is both manly and fatherly. I bathed my daughters, mixed their formula and fed them, changed their diapers, and took my turn getting up at night with them. It was a wonderful time of bonding. They came to accept my care as much as they did my wife's.

Many fathers fear handling a newborn, but it is easily learned. Babies are resilient. They have already survived birth; your awkward grasp won't disturb them very much. They don't break or crumble when touched or held. They tend to cuddle and cling.

It is a wonderful feeling when your baby snuggles up to you and reaches for your face. Experience it. Enjoy it. Let it bring your hearts together. Bonding at this age paves the way for bonding further down the path of maturity. Don't let your wife be the only one to experience this. Share with her in caring for your infant. She's had the child to herself for nine months. Now, insist on taking your turn.

BONDING DURING PRESCHOOL YEARS

It is almost unbelievable how rapidly your infant grows. Before long the baby is crawling on the floor, traveling about in the walker, then taking those first steps. It is a wonderful time of change, and you need to share in these changes. I know that the demands on your time are enormous, but budget your day to spend some time with your growing child. You might find it more rewarding than a golf game or a fishing trip. The child on the floor is a reproduction of you; that's a little version of you in the high chair. You now have a chance to relive your childhood through your own child.

When your child has learned the language, you can begin to see the world in a whole new way. Listen to those questions. Watch your child wonder at small things. Take your little one for a walk and watch what catches the child's interest. By sharing in that youthful perspective you will find excitement in things you have ignored for years.

Father God bonded with His preschool Son, Jesus:

When they [the wise men] had gone, an angel of the Lord appeared to Joseph in a dream. "Get up," he said, "take the child and His mother and escape to Egypt. Stay there until I tell you, for Herod is going to search for the child to kill Him."
Matthew 2:13

Some years later, this bonding continued:

After Herod died, an angel of the Lord appeared in a dream to Joseph in Egypt and said, "Get up, take the child and His mother and go to the land of Israel, for those who were trying to take the child's life are dead." Matthew 2:19-20

Father God was the Protector of His Son during Jesus' preschool years, and earthly fathers must be the protectors of their children during that time. Your children should feel absolutely safe and secure because of you. No worry should press upon them. In their beautiful innocence, let them enjoy life unencumbered by needless anxieties. Don't take their childhood away from them. They have only one chance at it.

It is amazing how much a child learns before starting school. Language, speech, walking, dressing, social manners, and going to the toilet are all learned in the home. Mothers and fathers are the main instructors. Let every opportunity of being with your child become a teaching experience. In a sense, you have a human computer in your home. Write the program you want your child to follow.

Fill your child with the Word of God in Bible stories, songs, Sunday school lessons, and Bible reading. If you can teach your children to tie their shoes, you can also teach the simple art of praying. Their little minds will never again find it easier to learn. Don't ignore this opportunity.

Teach your little preschooler the basic principles of morality. Children need to know the difference between right and wrong, and between yes and no. Show how to share and how to love. This is not textbook teaching, it is the sharing of a life. Children learn by listening and by watching you. What a wonderful bonding experience!

My Father and I

When the time comes for your child to begin school, you face a new set of challenges. Many parents who can afford it send their children to Christian schools, and a growing number of Christian parents are choosing to educate their children at home. Others send their children to public schools. When the time comes to release your child from the security of your home to go into the world of school, fear rises in your heart. You know the child will be exposed to some diverse philosophies of life and very different relationships with others. You are forced to allow strangers to teach your child, and you know it will mold the child's character and direct the child's future.

It is vital that you maintain a strong bond with your child during these years. Share in the schooling experience. Help with homework. Attend school functions with your child. Go with your wife to parent-teacher conferences. Learn what the teacher sees in your child, for the teacher sees things from an entirely different perspective than you do. Look through the teacher's eyes. Encourage your child and don't focus on weaknesses. Brag about your child's strengths and offer help to reinforce the weak places. Talk with your child about interpersonal relationships with the other students. Keep the bond you have built between yourselves strong during these years. Help your child to realize that the entire family backs the child throughout life.

Most gang activity exists as a substitute for strong home bonding. Although you probably cannot be your child's best friend, you can be a friendly father. You can be an advisor and source of security. You represent strength to your children, so don't let them down.

Make your child's activities an important part of your life. If your child is involved in sports, attend the games. If your child is in the school band or a drama club, go to the performances. These are important parts of a child's life. Share them, or you will find your children drifting away from you, and you'll wonder why there is such a gap between you. Never lose sight of the fact that you've been where your children are, but that they have not yet been where you are. Step backward in time and lead your child safely toward adulthood.

During the school years, don't neglect the spiritual life of your child. The public school systems offer little or no spiritual values. Often, humanistic teaching cuts across the grain of the spiritual standards by which we live. Reinforce your spiritual standards by praying with your children. Take them to Sunday school and church. Keep them involved in Christian youth activities. Help them realize that school is but a part of life; it is not their entire life.

It is interesting that Jesus was about twelve when He went to the Temple with His stepfather, Joseph.

Jesus became so engrossed in learning the Scriptures and the principles of the Jewish faith that He remained in the Temple three days after His parents had left for home. Joseph and Mary chided Him for remaining behind:

> *"Why were you searching for me?" He asked. "Didn't you know I had to be in My Father's house?"*   Luke 2:49

No matter what else this may teach us, it demonstrates that a twelve-year-old child has the capacity to understand Bible truths and the call of God upon our lives. Keep your children exposed to this kind of spiritual atmosphere. Bond with them in spiritual things.

And, Dad, don't let your son feel that spiritual things are feminine. Show him that men respond to God, too. Let him see in your life that godlikeness and manhood go hand in hand. Teach him to worship the Lord. Show him how to release his inner emotions to God in song and praise. If he sees you do it, he will do it. If you merely send him to church with his mother, it is unlikely that your son will ever become a worshiper of God. He needs to bond with you in worship. Help him!

BONDING THROUGHOUT LIFE

It may seem like an eternity from your child's birth until graduation from college or going into the workplace, but it will actually happen faster than you think possible. The cycle of life calls for your children to get out on their own, and often to become parents in their own right. This should not break the bond between you. It will be strengthened because it will have matured as the years pass.

When your child is making major decisions that will have an effect throughout life, you will have little direct input. You will have to trust the training and bonding of past years as, for example, you watch a daughter choose a lifetime partner in marriage. You can make recommendations and express your opinions, but basically, she will make the choice on her own. If you can gently guide without controlling, you can often prevent a serious mistake. If you are able to accept her choice and join in the joy of the marriage, your bonding will remain constant and may begin to affect her partner as he comes into the family.

Similarly, give as much counsel as will be accepted about choosing a career. It is not as common as it used to be for a son to walk in the footsteps of his father, nor is a daughter automatically slated to be a homemaker and wife. There are roles available to your children that were unavailable—even nonexistent—in past generations. Help your children explore these. Share with them in exploring the possibilities. Seeking knowledge together will help cement the bond between you.

Once your children are on their own, they still need a strong bond with their father. Didn't Father God recognize this? At the baptism of His Son, Jesus, His declaration of Jesus' sonship was also an expression of His approval.

Our adult children need our approval as well. I've just hung up the phone after a lengthy conversation initiated by my oldest daughter. She wanted to discuss her work and her relationship with her fellow workers. Although she is in her fifties, she needed reassurance and her father's approval. The bonding of years past makes me a security blanket and an emotional outlet for her in her mature years. And that's the way it should be. None of us walks through life alone. The more we maintain contact with close friends and parents, the safer we will be. Interestingly, we tend to reach back to those with whom we bonded early in life.

If you, the father, will bond with your children at the varying stages of life, you will remain their instructor throughout life.

SIX

A FATHER'S ROLE AS INSTRUCTOR

So Jesus said, "When you have lifted up the Son of Man, then you will know that I am the one I claim to be and that I do nothing on my own but speak just what the Father has taught me.

John 8:28

The wonder, the sense of mystery, and the feeling of creativity that overwhelmed you as a new father, when you initially held your newborn, were completely inexplicable. The baby's smile momentarily fulfilled every emotional need in your life. In your arms lay the most beautiful baby ever born into this world. Pride surged through you as though you had done this all by yourself. That's your baby!

As some of the euphoria drained away, you slowly began to realize that this miniature product of you and your wife was completely ignorant. Thousands of things that have become second nature to you are completely unknown to your child. Someone has a massive teaching job on his hands, and the initial responsibility does not belong to society or the church. This is a parental responsibility and you are one of the parents. What an awesome obligation!

How do you teach someone who knows nothing? It is like approaching a computer that lacks an operating system. This baby is a foreigner who has just arrived from the water world of the womb. Before birth he was fed through the umbilical cord, now, suddenly, he has to eat and digest food on his own. How can you help this little one bridge the distance? How can you, the father, teach this infant anything? It can be overwhelming to face this responsibility. Perhaps you can relax a little when you remember that Jesus said:

I do nothing on My own but speak just what the Father has taught Me.　　　　　　John 8:28

You can turn to our heavenly Father for help in teaching your child. Remember that one of the gifts of the Spirit is *"a word of knowledge"* (1 Corinthians 12:8, KJV).

God knows everything, and He makes what He knows available to us through His indwelling Spirit. The way we acquire knowledge from God is not unlike the way we use a laptop computer with a modem. The portable computer may have a screen ten inches or smaller, but it can tap into the vast information held in major mainframes across the country or around the world. It displays that knowledge one screenful at a time. Similarly, God gives us wisdom a word at a time, but that is probably all we can handle. It is all that our "screen" can hold. Once God has taught you, you can teach your child. The proper order is first prayer then teaching.

Perhaps the Holy Spirit should remind you that this was your own condition immediately following your conversion. You, too, were totally ignorant of spiritual things. You became the beneficiary of God's promise:

> *I will instruct thee and teach thee in the way which thou shalt go: I will guide thee with mine eye.*
> Psalm 32:8, KJV

This is the way you, the father, will teach your child. You will not necessarily have a classroom or textbooks. No computer program will assist you for the first few years. It will be a day-to-day, hour-by-hour, even moment-by-moment response to show your baby how to live. If you don't do it, someone else will. Will that someone teach your little one what you want your child to know, and teach by example about the kind of life you want your child to live?

We never completely outgrow our early instruction. Wise King Solomon said:

*Train a child in the way he should go, and when
he is old he will not turn from it.* Proverbs 22:6

In a very real sense, the way you bend your children in the early years will probably be the shape they will have throughout life, despite the influence of the educational systems. There will be a great gathering of information through the years, but all this knowledge will be processed through the principles you have taught in the early years of life. Yes, Dad, you do have a great responsibility on your hands.

Like your infant, Jesus did not come to Earth programmed with great knowledge. The record shows:

*And Jesus grew in wisdom and stature, and in
favor with God and men.* Luke 2:52

Jesus learned and developed intellectually, physically, and socially, and so must your child. But only the physical growth comes automatically. Wisdom and favor are acquired skills that need to be learned, and this requires a teacher. Who is more logical an instructor for these than you, Dad?

It is likely that Jesus learned much about natural living from His stepfather, Joseph, but Jesus learned His spiritual mission and ministry from His heavenly Father. Those long nights in prayer were learning sessions. Father God was the Instructor of His holy Son.

A Father's Role as Instructor

Not many fathers see themselves in the role of a teacher, but, like it or not, dads are instructors. It just goes along with the job. Your child will learn from you, whether or not you accept the responsibility of being an instructor. You may not choose to teach him, but your child will still choose to learn from you.

As your children relate to you, they learn about living through at least four methods:

1. Investigation: dad's supervision
2. Instruction: dad's communication
3. Association: dad's companionship
4. Discipline: dad's enforcement

FATHER, THE SUPERVISOR

It is almost beyond belief how much your baby will learn through investigation. While the baby is feeding, watch your child explore the surroundings with those little hands. Early learning comes through the sense of touch. Even before your child's eyes can focus clearly on objects, your baby will touch and taste anything in the immediate area.

When your baby is old enough to crawl on the floor, you will see everything going into that little mouth. You'll repeatedly say, "No, no!" and remove something from the baby's hand or mouth. Obviously, your baby doesn't know what is good to eat from what is not. Everything seems worth investigating, and that includes tasting. It is up to you and, of course, the mother to help the little one with this investigation.

Initially you put dangerous objects out of reach, but that tactic can't last forever. Your child needs your help in limiting investigation. The baby needs to learn to trust your judgment and to obey your "no-no" instructions. This requires tedious repetition on your part, and few babies automatically submit their wills to the will of Daddy. This is a learned response. The earlier you teach it, the easier it will be in the adolescent years.

At present, you may be stopping your child from putting pins, buttons, small objects, and anything unclean into that little mouth. Don't give up on this training. It can have life-long consequences. If the child learns to trust your supervision now, this trust should continue during the time the child stays under your jurisdiction. You are teaching now that the bar of soap in the bathtub does not go into the mouth. Later you can teach that cigarettes should never go into the mouth, either. If a child never tastes the first one, an appetite for the second one will never develop.

The same principle is true of drugs. If your children accept your supervision in small things, perhaps they will trust your restrictions on larger issues. When your children are tiny, you don't merely take something away; you offer a safe substitute. Your children need to realize that the purpose of your supervision is not to make life miserable, but to enable them to have a well-adjusted, happy life. You take away the dangerous thing and replace it with something that is safe and wholesome.

As your children grow older, your responsibility to guide their investigation moves from the mouth to the mind. They will need your supervision in controlling their thoughts and choosing what to dwell upon. Life will stimulate much thinking that will be unwholesome. Teach them what Paul taught the Christians at Philippi:

> *Whatever is true, whatever is noble, whatever is right, whatever is pure, whatever is lovely, whatever is admirable—if anything is excellent or praiseworthy—think about such things.*
>
> Philippians 4:8

You cannot keep your children from thinking and you wouldn't want to. But you can direct their thoughts into channels that will be positively productive. If they can learn to control their thoughts when they are children, they will carry that into adulthood.

Your children will not necessarily appreciate your role as a supervisor, but without guidelines and restrictions, they may very well self-destruct. As maturity develops, the amount of supervision may be reduced, but you will always be more experienced than your children. You may always need to take something out of their hands. Today it may be a pen; tomorrow it may be car keys. In either extreme, you may be seen as the bad guy, but it is a necessary part of your role as instructor in the home.

Investigation should not be repressed. It is a marvelous learning tool that needs to be used throughout life. Encourage it; direct it; and share in it. This is a big world that needs lots of investigation. Restrict this investigation to what is safe for the stage of maturity of your child, but don't repress the urge. This world is already far too full of people who have lost their desire to investigate.

Keep the curiosity of your children functioning as long as they are in your home. Don't let them settle for only television and video games. There is a wonderful world to be discovered in their own yard and neighborhood. Supervise them until good habits of investigation are automatic in their nature.

FATHER, THE COMMUNICATOR

The second way children learn is through instruction. Fortunately, your children will not learn only from mimicking you. Your children need to be told what to do. This is especially true in matters of motivation, morals, and manners. As valuable as the three R's are in life, the three M's form the foundation of life for your children. You dare not leave this instruction to modern society. These principles should be learned at home, and you, Dad, are the head of your home. You must talk to your children about behavior and beliefs. Remember, of course, that you cannot successfully instruct your children beyond your own level of living. Guard against the attitude of "Do as I say, not as I do."

Your children will not learn much about motivation, morals, and manners from formal instruction. They will learn these better from your informal conversations with them. Talk to them about life. Resist the urge to correct by saying, "Don't do that!" They will learn best when you can show them a better way to do, think, and behave.

Help keep your children correctly motivated. From time to time talk to them about why they do what they do. Help them learn that in God's sight, motivation is more important than manifestation. You'll be amazed at how often they don't really know why they do what they do. They may have acted out of impulse or instinct. Talk to them about it.

Sincere fatherly communication can keep your children motivated in school, sports, and life. You need not lecture, just communicate. Talk to them, and learn to listen to what they are saying. Keep your mind open to their opinions and thoughts; don't insist that your way is the only way. Make conversation a pleasant and natural part of your relationship. Day by day, teach them to remain correctly motivated. Don't let them drop out of life in childhood. Challenge them, encourage them, and direct their thinking. The more informally you can do this, the more effective you will be.

Your child was born a moral creature, possessing a soul. How each of us directs that soul depends upon the training we receive in our early life. You, Dad, need to determine the moral standard you want your children to have. Can you be satisfied with the modern standards of humanism? Are your children to live a self-centered life, with a constant drive for what they consider their rights? Today's world chooses to side step absolutes, and substitutes situation ethics that allow people to do whatever they feel comfortable with. Your children will be confronted with this attitude throughout most of their education. Can you live with this fact?

If you want the absolutes of God's Word to govern your children's morals, you must teach them. Don't depend on the church to do this; classroom moral instruction can be cold, formal, and detached. Your frank, comfortable, and frequent talks about morality will instill principles far deeper than classroom instruction will.

The innate curiosity of your children will open them very early to instruction about attitudes of the soul and spirit. The sooner you supply this information, the easier it will be. If you neglect this instruction, your children will pick up information from whatever source is available, whether it is right or wrong. Correcting this misinformation later in life may prove to be extremely difficult.

FATHER, THE COMPANION

A third way your children will learn to live is through association. Although there will always be a great distance in age and maturity levels, you can become a companion to your children. Invite them into your life. Do things with them. You can reach back to their level of maturity. Actually this can be rewarding, for it allows you to relive some of your childhood. Occasionally use your children as an excuse to be a boy again.

Earning a living in today's world demands a lot of your time and energy, but budget some time to be with your children. Play with them. Take them for walks. Hold them on your lap. Read to them. Tuck them into bed at night and tell them bedtime stories. They will be with you for such a short time. Make good use of that time.

As they mature, bring your children into your life more and more. Do you work at a job that will allow you to bring a child with you occasionally? They'll learn a great deal by seeing what you do to provide for them. Take them fishing with you, or maybe you can swim together. The more time you spend together, the greater the companionship will be. They will learn volumes just from being with you.

Last week I flew to a city in Missouri to minister in a church I had never before visited. On Saturday evening, I was taken directly from the airport to a restaurant where the entire church staff had gathered to get acquainted with me. The food was great, the fellowship was good, and the tension of not knowing one another greatly eased. Before the dessert was served, the pastor pushed back his chair, walked over to me and softly said, "Please excuse me. There is a hockey competition in town today, and my son's team is about to play. I need to be there for my son. I'll see you in the morning."

I was pleased that he gave his son priority over this social gathering. I doubt that this boy knows how fortunate he is to have such companionship with his dad. I do know that this relationship will make the next role of the father much easier.

FATHER, THE ENFORCER

Another method you must use to instruct your children is discipline. Rules imparted but not enforced will usually be ignored. It is not normal for your children to automatically want to do what you tell them to do. You will often have to compel them to follow the rules of the home. If they don't learn to submit to your authority, they won't submit to the authority governing their school or to the regulations controlling our society.

To many people, this statement of the writer to the Hebrews is disturbing:

> *Although He was a Son, He learned obedience from what He suffered.* Hebrews 5:8

It is difficult for any of us to believe that Jesus needed discipline to be an obedient son, but this is what the Scripture teaches. If God's Son needed discipline, your children certainly need it too.

Discipline is essential to learning, but discipline needs to be constant to be completely effective. You and your wife should agree on discipline. You should back one another in this. If you overrule your wife's discipline of your children, they will quickly learn to pit you against her to their advantage.

My wife and I always backed each other's disciplinary actions, even when we disagreed about it. We talked over our disagreement privately, and if some modification seemed in order, we let the person who had imposed the discipline rescind or adjust it.

Discipline should always be done in love, never in anger. The goal is not to punish, but to correct. The tone of voice will be authoritarian, but it need not be thunderous. Take a lesson from the police officer who pulls you to the curb for speeding. He doesn't yell, pull his gun, or rebuke you. He calmly tells you what you have done wrong and writes you a ticket. He is in authority and need not yell at you.

But as important as your discipline of your children is to their development into adulthood, it is even more important for you to teach your children to discipline themselves in life. They need to know that not everything in life will come automatically or easily. Some things your children learn through seeing. Other things are learned by hearing, but a vast amount of learning comes by doing. Playing the piano, for instance, cannot be learned by watching or by hearing about it. It requires the discipline of doing. Hours of practice precede success. It is rare for this discipline to be instinctive. It usually needs to be enforced.

My wife plays the guitar. When one of our grandsons took an interest in the instrument, she purchased a guitar for him and gave him lessons. We received letters telling of his great love for the instrument, and when we visited them for Christmas a few years later, Grandma encouraged him to bring out the guitar and play something for us. With great pride he began to strum absolute discord. He didn't know anything more about playing the guitar than the day she'd given him the instrument. He had never disciplined himself to practice what he had been taught (or at least what he had been told).

A Father's Role as Instructor

One of the greatest disciplines you can give your children is to instill in them the desire to read. Provide good books in the home. Teach your children to use the library. Challenge them to read. Set an example by reading in front of them. Read to your children, and have them read to you. Choosing the Bible for a daily reading adds a spiritual blessing. There is a whole world to be discovered through reading, but the nearly hypnotic pull of television keeps many children away from books. Discipline your children to limit their amusement time and to increase their enlightenment time. As it is said today, "A mind is a terrible thing to waste."

Also, teach your children the discipline of work. Many fathers who work long hours to supply their children with luxuries they never enjoyed are amazed that their children don't share their work ethic. Don't let this happen to you. The discipline of work is not in the genetic strain you passed on to your children at their conception. Work is a learned experience. You owe it to your children to teach them to accept the responsibility to work, and to find fulfillment and reward in it. This begins with chores and duties around the house. Later, let it extend to tasks in the neighborhood.

Also, don't just teach them to earn money; teach them to correctly use money and the discipline of saving money. Teach them to properly use a checking account. Help them to learn the convenience and the control of credit cards. Inform them that since money is in a foldable form, the way they use money reflects the attitude they have toward themselves. Impress upon them that money doesn't buy friends, and that they need to guard against letting others manipulate them into spending their money unwisely.

Teach your children the discipline of learning. The regimen of schooling must often be enforced. Left to themselves, many children would prefer to play video games and watch television programs than go to school and do homework. You need to teach your children that life is more than fun and games. If you don't teach it to them when they are small, society will harshly teach it to them later in life.

You may fear that discipline will break your child's spirit, but properly administered it will not break a spirit; discipline will channel it. The Bible assures us:

> *Folly is bound up in the heart of a child, but the rod of discipline will drive it far from him.*
>
> Proverbs 22:15

> *Do not withhold discipline from a child; if you punish him with the rod, he will not die.*
>
> Proverbs 23:13

Whatever this *"rod of correction"* means to you, it

is an obvious enforcing of the rules of the home. Don't sidestep this way of instruction.

You may never have a chalkboard in the home, and your classroom may be around the dining room table, but you and your wife are probably the best and most important teachers your children will ever have. Long after your children have forgotten what they learned in college, they will remember the practical principles they learned in the home, for those lessons were taught by demonstration, discipline, and loving talks during life experiences.

Dad, don't transfer the teaching of your children entirely to the professionals. Impart the fundamentals of Christian living to your children, and let the classroom instruction broaden and confirm what you have taught. If Father God took time to teach Jesus, surely we can find the time and strength to teach our sons and daughters. Remember that you have no options, for dads are instructors as much as they are patterns.

CHAPTER

SEVEN

A FATHER'S ROLE AS EXAMPLE

"I am one who testifies for myself; my other witness is the Father, who sent me." Then they asked him, "Where is your father?" "You do not know me or my Father," Jesus replied. "If you knew me, you would know my Father also." John 8:18-19

When the religious rulers pressed Jesus to verify that He was the Son of God, this was His reply. What a beautiful testimony! Jesus' Father was so much the pattern of His life that He dared say, *"If you knew Me, you would know My Father also."* Good patterns and good craftsmen make good products.

A craftsman studies his pattern carefully, for the commodity he is about to make will be an extension of that design. If the pattern is flawed, the product will be imperfect. Similarly, a wise young woman looks well and long at the man to whom she is attracted, for she knows that he may become not only the biological father of her children, but the pattern for their lives as well. What that man is will have more authority in the lives of his children than anything he says. We know that what we do speaks so loudly that people sometimes can't hear what we say, and that this is never more true than in our relationship with our children. What do your children hear when looking at you, Dad?

Howard Hendricks tells us, "In a barber shop recently I struck up a conversation with a boy I'd seen there before. After a while I asked, 'Who do you want to be like?' 'Mister,' he said, 'I ain't found nobody I want to be like.' "[2]

That boy was not an exception. If you're out there in the battle, you know what I'm talking about. Kids aren't looking for a perfect teacher—just an honest one and one they can respect. Yet, for so may of them, the pedestals are empty.

Dads, we are the pattern for the lives of our children. They will become an extension of our lives into the next generation. Even if you have lacked a good earthly example for being a father, look to your heavenly Father. At least twice Jesus suggested that we model our lives after Father God. He said:

Be perfect, therefore, as your heavenly Father is perfect.   Matthew 5:48

Be merciful, just as your Father is merciful.
                                        Luke 6:36

May God give us the grace to be enough like our heavenly Father that our children will want to be like us. Just as we need God for our example, our children desperately need us for a role model.

Jesus said:

> *I speak that which I have seen with My Father: and ye do that which ye have seen with your father.* John 8:38, KJV

If Jesus took His Father as the pattern for His life, we can expect our children to take us, their fathers, as the model for their lives. It really is not so much a choice our children make as it is a natural response to association with the highest authority figure in their young lives.

Some of the patterns we fathers become in our children are genetic. They often look like us, walk like us, and do things the way we do, long before they could consciously copy us. We sometimes pity them for having no choice but to be so much like us, but that is the material of which they were formed. They did not choose the pattern; we did.

The reverse to this is that we often see what we really are by looking closely at our children. Their actions and their attitudes sometimes give us unwanted insights into ourselves. Dad, you'll find it painful to spank your children for doing something you yourself still do. In correcting them, you'll need to correct yourself, for you are their pattern of behavior.

My Father and I

Several years ago, *Christian Life and Faith* magazine presented some unusual facts about two families. In 1677 an immoral man married a very licentious woman. Nineteen hundred descendants came from the generations begun by that union. Of these, 771 were criminals, 250 were arrested for various offenses, 60 were thieves, and 39 were convicted for murder. Forty of the women were known to have venereal disease. These people spent a combined total of 1,300 years behind bars and cost the State of New York nearly $3 million.

The other family was the Edwards family. The third generation included Jonathan Edwards, the great New England revival preacher who became president of Princeton University. Of the Edwards family's 1,344 descendants, many were college presidents and professors. One hundred eighty-six became ministers of the Gospel, and many others were active in their churches. Eighty-six were state senators, three were congressmen, thirty were judges, and one became Vice President of the United States. No reference was made to anyone's spending time in jail or in the poorhouse. [3]

Not all children of good parents become useful citizens, nor do all the offspring of wicked people turn out bad. Yet the possibility of a child's getting the right start in life is improved if the child comes from a home where love prevails, the Bible is taught, and prayer is offered.

A Father's Role as Example

Dad, when you live for the Lord, you provide a strong incentive for your children to choose the Christian way of life. Parental example is extremely powerful—either for good or for evil. You need to remind yourself that you do not live for yourself alone. You are also continuing to live through your children, and, because of that, the way you live will affect future generations.

Beyond being a genetic pattern for your children, there are at least three other areas where you become a pattern, particularly for your sons. To them you will be:

1. A pattern of manhood
2. A pattern of manners
3. A pattern of morality

FATHER, THE PATTERN OF MANHOOD

Whether you like it or not, you are a visual pattern of manhood to your son. There is great confusion in our Western society about the role of men. Television often paints the picture of the father as a wimp or a weakling. Hollywood, on the other hand, almost deifies the image of man as a fighter or superhero, with great powers of destruction. Somewhere between these two extremes of weakness and strength lies the true image of a man. A good man is both strong and tender. He is authoritarian, but he is loving. He is a producer and also a provider. He is methodical, but he is also emotional. He is a leader who can be led.

The Bible reports:

> *So God created man in His own image, in the image of God He created him; male and female He created them. God blessed them and said to them, "Be fruitful and increase in number; fill the earth and subdue it. Rule over the fish of the sea and the birds of the air and over every living creature that moves on the ground."*   Genesis 1:27-28

In this simple statement, we see at least four characteristics that constitute manhood:

1. Sexuality
2. The image of God
3. The ability to exercise dominion
4. The capacity to accept responsibility

The first of these is often viewed as the primary mark of manhood—sexuality. Although it is true that God commanded the man and woman to reproduce and populate the Earth, this is not the most important measure of manhood. Teenagers can sexually reproduce themselves, as can most animals, birds, and fish. It is amusing to watch a man parade his masculinity, based on his sexual prowess, when we all realize that the woman in his life actually controls the expression of that sexual drive. God put reproductive systems into both Adam and Eve, not merely into Adam.

The second characteristic of manhood is that of being formed in the image of God. This is far more the mark of manhood than anything else. No other creature on Earth was formed by the finger of God. God spoke the other creatures into existence. Man and woman alone were formed by God's hand and given life by the breath of God. We read:

> *The LORD God formed the man from the dust of the ground and breathed into his nostrils the breath of life, and the man became a living being.*
> Genesis 2:7

Both your son and daughter need to see this God-like quality in your life. You reflect the image of God, although unfortunately sin has greatly marred and defaced that image in all of us. God has made provision for our redemption:

> *He saved us through the washing of rebirth and renewal by the Holy Spirit.* Titus 3:5

By placing His Holy Spirit within us, God has endowed us with His image. Radiate that divine image. Let God's presence be seen in your speech, your motives, your morals, and your behavior. Especially let it be seen by your children.

The third thing God said He gave to man was the ability to exercise dominion. Adam's dominion was absolute. Ours is limited. Still, a true man maintains dominion over himself—over his spirit, soul, and body. Show your son that you are not controlled by your body; you have dominion over it. Let him see that your will and emotions do not completely rule you; you rule them. Teach him that, like you, he can have dominion over feelings, attitudes, likes, and dislikes.

Adam was to have dominion over his world, and so should we. God has given us rulership and dominion over our world—our home, our children, our sphere of influence. This, of course, does not authorize any man to become lord and king in his household; rather he is its guide, counselor, and top authority. Someone has to be in charge of the home (not just in authority over it, but in the care of it), and God has given the man that role. The buck has to stop somewhere just to maintain the peace of the home. Dad, the buck—the responsibility—stops with you.

The fourth, and perhaps most distinguishing, characteristic of a true man is his capacity to accept responsibility. God turned the care of the garden over to Adam, and God trusted him to follow through with this responsibility. A true man can carry responsibility with great grace.

Many men of our generation will not accept responsibility. They run from it. Even after they secure employment, they have a high rate of absenteeism. They run up debts, but they do not pay. They marry, but they do not support their wives. Often when pregnancy is announced, they flee to the next town. They may be males, but they are not men in the biblical sense. You don't want your son to be like that. Demonstrate a man's ability to accept responsibility.

By your example, teach your son to be accountable. Accountability needs to be learned early. You are his prime example of manhood. Demonstrate true manhood to your family in the home. Demonstrate your willingness to be responsible in every area of your marriage.

If this pattern seems too difficult to measure up to, remember that Jesus fit it perfectly. None has borne the image of God as He did. No man has ever demonstrated such dominion and authority over nature, demons, sickness, and death. Where can we find a man who was more responsible than Jesus? He deliberately set His face to go to the cross, even though people were willing to make Him their earthly king.

This perfect example became God's last Adam. Paul explained:

*The first man Adam became a living being; the
last Adam, a life-giving spirit.*

1 Corinthians 15:45

Jesus did perfectly all that Adam had failed to do,
and He became a *"life-giving spirit"* in the process.
In areas where you feel you are failing as a pattern
of manhood, come to Jesus for a renewal by His
Spirit.

Girls tend to expect all men in their lives to be
like their father, and boys use their father's image
as the model for manhood. In marriage counseling,
I have frequently found the crux of the problem in a
marriage has been the male image that the father
created in his daughter by the way he treated her as
she was growing up. This was now her image of
men, and she projected it onto her husband—
whether it fit or not. Right or wrong, good or bad,
we dads create a lifetime image of manhood in our
children.

Similarly, I have seen young men become poor
husbands because of the pattern they had seen in
their fathers. The son responded to his wife very
much as he had seen his father relate to the mother,
for this was viewed as an acceptable standard of
conduct.

Edgar Guest wrote:

*I'd rather see a sermon than hear one any day;
I'd rather one should walk with me than merely*

show the way;

For the eye's a better pupil and more willing than the ear;

Good counsel is confusing but examples always clear.

And best of all the preachers are the men who live their creeds;

For to see good put into action is what everybody needs.

I can soon learn how to do it if you let me see it done;

I can watch your hands in action, but your tongues too fast may run.

And the lectures you deliver may be very fine and true,

But I'd rather get my lesson by observing what you do;

For I may misunderstand you and the high advice you give,

But there's no misunderstanding how you act and how you live. [4]

We not only form the mental pattern of masculinity by our lives, but we also become the standard pattern of behavior for our children.

FATHER, THE PATTERN OF MANNERS

For the first five years of life, most of what a child learns is through observation and association. Dad is usually the great hero in the home, and everything he does is seen as wonderful. Children try desperately to copy his actions, speech, and mannerisms. At times this can be comical to watch. At other times, it is almost devastating.

What we dads do around our children forms an indelible pattern of manners in their minds. This was exemplified by a father and son visiting in the home of a business associate of the father.

"What will you have to drink?" the host asked.

"I'll take what Father takes," the son replied.

The thought of his responsibility gripped the father, who answered, "I'll take water."

Another choice might have sent his son to a drunkard's grave.

Children, especially boys, love to do what their father does. If he smokes, they can hardly wait to get their hands on a cigarette. If Dad is a beer drinker, his son will probably begin drinking beer before he is legally old enough to do so. It seems so smart to be like Daddy.

Although it is likely that you want your son to become a better man than you are, children learn from role models, and you, Dad, are the most important role model in your son's life. Your son not only has your genes in him, he has your lifestyle in front of him. No wonder people say that he is "a chip off the old block."

Jesus let His Father be His role model. He admitted:

A Father's Role as Example

*I do nothing on My own but speak just what the
Father has taught Me.*   John 8:28

God must have been an excellent teacher, since
Jesus was a perfect example while He was here on
Earth.

Your child is more apt to be like you than to be
like his teachers or those in his peer group, for you
made lasting impressions on him when he was in
his most formative stages. When clay is soft, a gentle
pressure makes a deep impression, but when the
clay hardens, it takes a sharp cutting instrument to
make the same mark. You have the first chance to
mark your son, and whether you realize it or not,
you do leave your mark.

While a boy is in his preschool years, he views
his Dad as his superhero. This is especially true if
the wife is openly expressive of her love for her husband. On a scale of 1 to 10, most sons place Dad at
11 or higher. Someone has wisely prayed, "Lord,
help me to be the man my son thinks I am!"

Your children will pick up attitudes toward life
from watching your behavior in the home. For instance, your son will develop his attitude toward
women from watching the way you treat his mother.
If you treat her as a servant, he will develop an attitude of superiority over women. When you accept
her as your equal and flow together in love as a team,
this will become the aspiration for his marriage.

Similarly, if you physically abuse your wife, your son will likely abuse the women who enter his life.

Because this principle is seldom reversed, every young woman would do herself a great service by observing the way the young man of her affections treats his mother and the way the parents relate to one another before accepting an engagement ring. Marriage is not likely to change the young man's attitude toward women. He will probably treat his wife as his father treats his mother.

Your children, and sons especially, will function in the home much as they see you function. If you never help around the house, your son will resist doing chores. If you are a workaholic who is seldom home, as he grows older your son will stay away from the house. If you become a TV couch potato, so will he. It is not so much a deliberate attempt to pattern himself after you as it is a subconscious response to what he consistently sees in you.

A son likes to wear his father's shirts, shoes, and anything else he can get his hands on. It doesn't matter if the clothing is hopelessly too large; he is playing the role of the daddy. I sometimes saw myself in ways I had never seen before by watching my daughters pretend they were me. Occasionally it was shocking, often it was amusing, but always it was informative.

Someone has written:

A Father's Role as Example

*There's a wide-eyed little youngster who believes
you're always right;
And his ears are always open, and he watches day
and night;
You are setting an example every day in all you
do,
For the little one who's watching to grow up and
be like you!* [5]   —Author unknown

Dad is the prime example of dress, table manners, hospitality, and personal care for his sons. If you don't pick up after yourself, you will find it difficult to teach your son to keep his room in order. It is difficult to teach your son to eat like a gentleman—if your table manners are atrocious. If you are curt to strangers and cold to a guest who comes to your house, you can expect the same behavior in your son. If you are warm, friendly, and able to put guests at ease around you, your son will likely develop the same traits. In a hundred other ways, what you say will be far less important than what you do. What your boy sees in you is more powerful in teaching him than what he hears from you. He will be *like* you far more than he will listen *to* you.

Dads, our sons not only tend to fashion their social graces according to the pattern they see in our lives, but they also pick up our behavior in the handling of money. The father who consistently mortgages his future to finance his present will usually have children who face adulthood with credit cards "maxed out." Happy is the child who learns financial discipline from watching his dad.

Your behavior in times of crisis also becomes a pattern for your son. When you respond in faith, your son learns dependence upon God's provision, but when you respond in fear, he easily becomes fearful in facing life. If negative circumstances cause bitter reactions in you, they will later cause similar bitter reactions in your son. If you blame your mother or wife or others for your "bad luck," your son will learn to divorce himself from personal responsibility and blame others too.

It is not by accident that Paul challenged Titus:

In everything set them an example by doing what is good. In your teaching show integrity, seriousness and soundness of speech that cannot be condemned, so that those who oppose you may be ashamed because they have nothing bad to say about us.   Titus 2:7-8

True teaching is far more "show" than "tell." Dads, your children are watching you; they listen to what you say. As they mature, they may reject your behavior as being unfit for their lives, but this usually includes a rejection of dad as well.

A Father's Role as Example

FATHER, THE PATTERN OF MORALITY

Good moral standards are better caught than taught. All the lecturing in the world cannot overcome what children see in the father. You are a pattern of either good or bad principles to your children. If you can't be trusted to keep your word, they will follow your pattern of lying. If they see you cheating others, they themselves will become cheats.

Sons will handle their developing sexuality according to what they have seen in Dad's life far more than by what they have seen on television or in the lives of others. Dad, you are the prime example for your son. You may think he is unaware of your philandering, and your wife may deliberately pretend that all is well between you, but children have a sixth sense that sees through sham and hypocrisy far better than most of us realize.

Children are sensitive to emotions in the home, and they are very observant of actions outside the home. When you live in sexual purity, your son will see this as the proper standard for life. When he sees you restrict your sexuality to your relationship with your wife, he sees this as the normal relationship in a marriage. This will be his inner pattern of true morality in sexual ethics. Of course, you will talk to your son about his sexuality, but he will learn far more about it from observing you.

Your children will learn a work ethic both by what

you teach and what you do. Your example of faithful work, day in and day out, gives them a powerful insight into what is in store for life later on. Your attitude toward your job will probably instill in them a similar attitude about work. Help them to realize that no job need be degrading.

The sixteenth president of the United States, Abraham Lincoln, said, "My father taught me to work, but not to love it. I never did like to work, and I don't deny it. I'd rather read, tell stories, crack jokes, talk, laugh—anything but work." However, look at what this man accomplished with his life. What if his father had not taught him the discipline of work?

Please accept the fact that the public schools will not teach your son or daughter the basic moral principles of life. Since we have ruled religion out of the educational system, it is virtually impossible for them to teach morals—even if they wanted to. Lord Devlin in his work The Enforcement of Morals said:

> *"No society has yet solved the problem of how to teach morality without religion. So the law must base itself on Christian morals and to the best of its ability enforce them, not simply because they are the morals of most of us, nor simply because they are the morals taught by the established Church—on these points the law recognises the right to dissent—but for the compelling reason that without the help of Christian teaching the law will fail."* [6]

130

A Father's Role as Example

This means, Dad, that you will fail in being the pattern of morality for your children unless you are also a pattern for spirituality to your children. The Word of God has to have meaning for you before it will have meaning for them. Divine principles need to be worked out in your life if you want to see them exemplified in the life of your sons and daughters.

Let your children see you reading your Bible and praying from time to time. For most of us men, this is a private activity, but our children need to be let in on it once in a while. Better yet, share your Bible reading with them. Read the Bible to them, and have them read it to you. It is healthy for this to be a regular activity. As your little ones get older, ask them questions about the Bible, and let them ask you questions about what you have read to them.

There is no more practical tool for teaching moral living than the Book of Proverbs. How about letting a verse from this book of wisdom precede or follow the prayer over the evening meal? Maybe, while you are eating, you can discuss what the verse means. It will give you an opportunity to teach a moral standard before it is broken. It is always better to prevent than to punish. Children hear better when they are not struggling with guilt feelings.

You, dear Dad, are automatically a pattern for your children. Whether you are conscious of it or not, you are a pattern of behavior for your children from birth to death. You are also their source of provision.

EIGHT

A FATHER'S ROLE AS PROVIDER

*So, and because Jesus was doing these things on
the Sabbath, the Jews persecuted Him. Jesus said
to them, "My Father is always at His work to this
very day, and I, too, am working."* John 5:16-17

After the birth of Jesus, God didn't merely sit back
and watch events; He went to work. Jesus could con-
fidently say, *"My Father is always at His work to this
very day,"* and happy is the child who can say the
same thing. Dad's faithfulness to go to work is a
strong source of security for the family. In today's
society, it is often necessary for both mother and father to go to work daily to maintain the standard of
living they have become accustomed to or just to
provide the basics of life.

Some people in my generation viewed work as
an intrusion into their lifestyle. They denounced material things and claimed to need nothing; therefore,
they refused to work. Most of them lived off the labor of others and learned to work the governmental
system of obtaining free help and grants. Even many
who came to Christ expected the church to support

them while they sat around reading their Bibles and sleeping in the church basement.

God has ordained that the leaders of the household work. Paul told the saints at Thessalonica:

> *For even when we were with you, we gave you this rule: "If a man will not work, he shall not eat."*   2 Thessalonians 3:10

This great apostle did not feel that able-bodied persons had a right to live off another's toil. Each should provide his own living.

This rule of life was not merely to spare society from freeloaders. Paul realized that work is God's provision to give a person a sense of purpose and fulfillment. Work is not a "necessary evil." Those who see work as part of God's curse upon man for sinning overlook God's provision during the time of Adam's innocence. The record shows:

> *The LORD God took the man and put him in the Garden of Eden to work it and take care of it.*
> Genesis 2:15

God gave Adam the Garden of Eden, and Adam was expected to tend it. Adam was the world's first farmer. God's original plan, even before creation, was that His creatures should find fulfillment in work. The old cliche' "Idleness is the devil's workshop," is based upon astute observation. Laziness and inactivity are never God's will for a healthy person.

More than that, the Bible says:

If anyone does not provide for his relatives, and especially for his immediate family, he has denied the faith and is worse than an unbeliever.

1 Timothy 5:8

A father must provide for more than his own living; he is expected to provide a living for the members of his household. The New Testament makes no room for a lazy father. It teaches that a Christian father who refuses to work to support his family is counted by God as an unbeliever. His works are inharmonious with his professed faith.

A FATHER MUST PROVIDE THE FINANCES FOR HIS FAMILY

Dad, sometimes you may feel unspiritual because you cannot attend the daytime church functions your wife attends (if she has no job outside the home), and you have so much less time to read the Bible and pray than she does. Do you realize that your faithful attention to providing for the needs of your family is worship in the eyes of God? It is God's way of providing for the needs of others through your hands.

Many years ago I clipped out an item by Harry Emerson Fosdick and placed it in the front of my Bible as a gentle reminder. He wrote:

> *A dollar is a miraculous thing. It is a man's personal energy reduced to portable form and endowed with powers the man himself does not possess. It can go where he cannot go; speak languages he cannot speak; lift burdens he cannot touch with his fingers; save lives with which he cannot directly deal—so that a man busy all day downtown can at the same time be working in boys' clubs, hospitals, settlements, children's centers all over the city.* [7]

In faithfully working at your job, you are living in obedience to the Word of God and are doing for your family what God the Father does on our behalf—working. He works! He provides for our needs! He is our prime example of unselfishness.

Working to gain money and learning to properly use what you earn is not inherent to human nature. It is a learned experience. Consider the saga of another young man: When he graduated from high school, his mother gave him the most beautiful leather wallet he had ever seen. As a young man living at home, everything he earned went into that wallet; there was no bank account for this lad. When he felt the money in the fat wallet in his hip pocket, he knew it was all his, and it gave him a feeling of security. The wallet supported his car and financed all his fun and games. He and the wallet became inseparable as the years passed.

This young man was beginning to discover that money was himself in foldable form. He exchanged brains or brawn for a medium called money. When he earned ten dollars an hour, every ten-dollar bill in his wallet represented an hour of his labor. This dad-in-the-making was not in love with his wallet; he was in love with himself. He had himself safely tucked away in his wallet.

When he fell hopelessly in love and found it necessary to share the contents of that wallet with a wife, it wasn't as severe as he first feared, for his bride brought her wallet into the marriage, and they shared. His wallet slimmed down after the wedding, but it was still his.

With the arrival of each child into his life, the wallet deflated like a punctured balloon and sat in his pocket as flat as a pancake. What had once been exclusively *his* rapidly became community property. All the members of the household had their hands in his wallet. Dad was learning to give his life to the family. The wallet's condition was now the same as when it had been received—empty!

Jesus told His disciples:

All that belongs to the Father is Mine.

John 16:15

God the Father shared everything He had with His Son. He accepted the responsibility of making provision for Jesus. He maintained an open wallet with Him, and so must we in our time. We must consistently share with our children what we possess so they will lack nothing needed for their maturing. We must give them more than biological life; we must give everything necessary to keep sustaining that life.

Now let us return to our young dad. He had once seen his wallet as a provider for his own wants. After the children came into his life, however, he began to see that piece of leather as an instructor. It would teach him many things about life. He would learn that his wallet:

1. Deals with past selfishness.
2. Deals with present dependence.
3. Deals with predetermined planning.

Initially, the most difficult part of marriage is handling selfishness. It is the part of our childhood that refuses to leave voluntarily, for it is a vital part of our sinful nature. The prophet Isaiah said:

> *All we like sheep have gone astray; we have turned every one to his own way; and the LORD hath laid on Him the iniquity of us all.* Isaiah 53:6, KJV

A Father's Role as Provider

The heart of sin involves insisting on having our own way, and we dads certainly bring that into our marriages.

One of God's ways of making us aware of our selfishness is through our wallets. These wonderful deposits of our past endeavors no longer belong to us exclusively. They must be shared with our growing family. There are mortgage payments to be met, utility bills to be paid, car payments to be made in addition to the sharing of money for food, clothes, and recreation for someone besides ourselves. Someone has wisely said that more men will embrace a woman than will embrace mortgage payments.

As Dad learns to be more and more selfless, he often begins to grasp the tremendous price Jesus paid to bring us to spiritual maturity. Jesus selflessly laid aside all His heavenly splendor, position, power, and majesty to reach down to meet our needs. Heaven's wallet was made available to us. God's divine provision became a saving grace to us. What an example!

As Dad works harder and longer to try to keep some money in his wallet, that graduation gift from his mother begins to deal with present dependence. It can be a crushing load for a young father when it really dawns on him that absolutely everything his children will need in the coming days and years must come out of his wallet—and his wife's, if she has a job outside the home. The children are utterly and completely dependent upon the parents as their only resource.

When my children were small, they would begin to hint for money as we approached certain special events such as Mother's Day, Father's Day, birthdays, or Christmas. I knew they wanted funds to purchase gifts, and since my wife didn't work outside the home, I was their only source of supply. I gave to them so that they were able to give to others. Through this I learned that in order to have anything to give to God, I had to come to God to receive it, for He is my only Source of spiritual life. Oh, what lessons the wallet can teach a dad!

That folded piece of leather in the young dad's back pocket also deals with predetermined planning. Originally the wallet was merely concerned with today. It directed Dad's life as though there would be no tomorrow. But the owner is no longer a teenager now. He is a father. He has learned to put away his selfishness and deal with the dependence of others on his provision. Now this dad needs to learn to plan in the present for the future of his family.

He faces the need for insurance, just in case something happens to him. He needs to recognize that the little child learning to feed himself at the table will soon need to go to college to learn a skill. In today's economy, money for education is a major expense—too large an amount to be raised in a short period of time. The money must be saved before the children reach college age.

Dad's depreciating wallet also warns him that it is necessary to set some money aside for emergencies, for they will come. Dad can either plan ahead or forever be borrowing against his future to meet current expenses.

It may have been a love gift from his mother, but this father's wallet became a tool in the hand of God to teach him many lessons about his relationship to others and his dependence on God. Thank God for wallets!

The above scenario is, of course, the ideal. It assumes an income that continues to increase as the young father matures in his trade or calling. Unfortunately, life does not always follow ideal patterns. Children come to the day laborer as well as to the corporation CEO. Not all fathers will be able to do all they would like to do for their children. This should not be a basis for guilt or condemnation. The principle is to recognize that the needs of our children will be met by their fathers. We are not expected to give what we do not possess, but we are expected to share as abundantly as possible for the children in the present and to make as good an investment in their future as feasible.

A FATHER PROVIDES THE FINANCIAL SECURITY FOR HIS FAMILY

Happy is the home where the father gives a sense of security as the provider. No matter what his own insecurities may be, he dare not project them to the family. Children need to feel that nothing necessary will be denied them. A dad's insecurities should be taken to the Lord, not to his family.

It is difficult to provide financial security for the family if you are insecure financially yourself. This really has little to do with the amount of money you have. It is far more a matter of how you manage that money. It is not the money that flows through your checking account that matters as much as the amount that remains there at the end of the month. Controlling your cash flow is the secret to financial security. There are at least six foundational steps to help you gain and maintain control of your money:

1. Developing a credible budget
2. Using credit restrictions
3. Implementing cash-basis living
4. Developing the discipline of constant savings
5. Securing comfortable insurance
6. Obeying God in consistent giving

Take a brief look at these six steps before rejecting them. They are not complex, but they are wonderfully releasing. Although some anxieties can be released through prayer, financial anxieties are best prevented by preparation.

The first step is to develop a credible budget, and then make yourself live within that budget. Without a budget you may easily find yourself out of control in impulse buying. A budget helps your left hand know what the right hand is doing. It also lets both hands know that some things just cannot be done this month or next. The purpose of a budget is not to restrict and repress; it is to direct and discipline you in handling your money. There are books on the market that will help you develop your budget, and from time to time seminars are held to give you personal guidance in building a budget. Use these resources.

A second step to gain control of your finances is the use of credit restrictions. Credit is a wonderful servant, but it is a cruel master. Learn to severely control your use of credit. Nothing will erode your financial security faster than borrowing on future income to live in the present. You and your wife need to work closely together to limit credit purchases. Plastic cards are a convenience, but they are easily abused.

People are funny; they spend money they don't have, to buy things they don't need, to impress folks they don't like. And they use their credit to finance this foolishness. At the time of the writing of this book, Americans owe over $3 billion to credit card companies, and they will pay in excess of $360 million in interest annually. [8] This is a serious mortgage on our future, and it is severely limiting our enjoyment of the present.

Dad, learn to control your pride and lust when making major purchases. Do you and the family really need this latest purchase? Or do you just merely want it? Could the needed item be purchased secondhand? Much of the time, used items purchased for cash are preferable to new items purchased on credit. That new item is going to be classified as "used" right after you get it home anyway, but the payments go on and on, eroding your income.

The third step to financial security may seem un-American, but every American Christian must learn to do it. Set a goal to get onto a cash basis and stay there. Few Americans know the freedom and liberty that being debt-free brings to life. We have become too accustomed to borrowing against our future to receive present gratification. We forget that borrowing makes the lender the controller of our lives.

Except for house payments, my wife and I have lived debt-free for more than thirty years. We do not live with a mortgaged future. We use credit cards strictly as a convenience. If we don't have money in the bank to pay the card purchase, we delay buying until we do. When the bill comes due, we pay the total balance each month. We enjoy the liberty this has given to our lives.

It may take you a year or two to pay off what you secured in your past by borrowing against your future, but the peace of mind it will bring will be more than worth it. Try it! You will again gain control of your life.

A fourth step to financial security is to develop the discipline of constant saving. An old Amish proverb says, "Spend less than you earn and you'll never be in debt." It sounds so simple, but today it is easier said than done. It can be done, however, and it needs to be done.

No matter how small your income may be or how high living expenses soar as the baby arrives in the home, a portion of every check should go into some form of savings. Life is full of surprises. Emergencies come at the most inopportune times. If you haven't been putting money aside, you'll have to borrow money to meet those emergencies, and the interest you will pay will greatly increase the cost.

Remind yourself that if your budget can handle those credit payments that will follow emergencies, it can handle that same amount in savings. Why not let the bank pay you interest instead of constantly paying interest to the bank yourself? If you find it difficult to actually put cash into a savings account, most banks will automatically deduct a set amount from your checking account into a savings account for you.

A fifth way to undergird your sense of financial security is to carry enough insurance to supply the family in the event of their losing you. Don't become insurance poor; be insurance secure. Most of us expect to live to an old age, but we have no promise of this. Anything you can do to secure your family's future will give you inner security, and you will project this to your family.

The sixth step to developing an inner security in your finances is constant giving. Never forget that a clenched fist cannot receive anything. The wise man wrote:

> *A generous man will prosper; he who refreshes others will himself be refreshed.* Proverbs 11:25

Giving should always begin with the minimum of a tithe (ten percent) of your income given back to God. This is the rent we pay for living and working on the Earth. In the final book of the Old Testament, God challenged the people He had released from slavery in Babylon:

> *Bring ye all the tithes into the storehouse, that there may be meat in Mine house, and prove Me now herewith, saith the LORD of hosts, if I will not open you the windows of heaven, and pour you out a blessing, that there shall not be room enough to receive it.* Malachi 3:10, KJV

You may argue with this if you choose, but millions of people have entered into a tithing covenant with God and found Him more than willing to keep His part of the contract. As we give Him what He claims as His, He abundantly shares with us what He holds as His own.

People have often told me that they just cannot afford to tithe. I have insisted that they cannot afford *not* to tithe. It is a divine principle that consistently works. Jesus taught us:

> *Give, and it shall be given unto you; good measure, pressed down, and shaken together, and running over, shall men give into your bosom. For with the same measure that ye mete withal it shall be measured to you again.* Luke 6:38, KJV

If we are stingy, we will receive a meager reward. If we are liberal in our giving, God will be generous to us.

DAD, YOU'RE NOT ALONE

As the family believes that Dad will supply all their needs, so you, Dad, need to remember the words of the New Testament:

> *And my God will meet all your needs according to His glorious riches in Christ Jesus.*
> Philippians 4:19

As others become comfortable in their dependence upon you, you need to become comfortable in your dependence upon your heavenly Father. Your children may think that you are an inexhaustible source of supply, but you know that it is your Father in Heaven whose bank account is never drained. Often what you need in order to provide security for the family is beyond your and your wife's current abilities. You need outside help. Jesus knew this, so He said:

> *In that day you will no longer ask Me anything. I tell you the truth, My Father will give you whatever you ask in My name.*   John 16:23

God's gifts don't always come in the form of a check. Sometimes they come as an inspiration or an energy to work beyond past performance. At other times, God opens opportunities far different from what has been available before. God does not usually replace our work with a blank check, but He can and will direct us into activities that prove very profitable. It reminds us of one of Paul's observations:

> *As God's fellow workers we urge you not to receive God's grace in vain.*   2 Corinthians 6:1

The King James Version says that we are *"workers together with Him."* Dad, you really are not on your own. Your heavenly Father stands by to undergird you with His wisdom, encouragement, and resources, but He needs you to work with Him in securing and managing the resources your family needs.

A FATHER PROVIDES EMOTIONAL STABILITY FOR HIS FAMILY

The interaction of members in the home often produces tension. Like a car coasting down hill in neutral, these tensions pick up increasing speed until they often crash disastrously in open confrontation. The home needs a referee, and Dad is nominated.

Maybe you don't wear a striped shirt like the referee at a football game, but you are outside the game of the home all day long, so you are the controller. When you arrive home, you are often called upon to be the justice of the peace before you get your coat hung up. Perhaps your wife, in desperation, has told the children, "Just wait until your father gets home." They wait, but in tension and apprehension. When you arrive home, you sense emotional stress immediately. You can either explode, or defuse those emotions.

You may have had a rough day at work. You may be emotionally stirred because of interaction at the job. Don't mix your emotions from work with the emotions in the home. Remember what your heavenly Father told you:

*A gentle answer turns away wrath, but a harsh
word stirs up anger.*   Proverbs 15:1

Never forget that the one in authority need not
yell.

There will be other days when the mood of the
home will be dark, and depression will seem to
reign. The easiest way out is to run. Playing a game
of golf will help you escape the mood in the home,
but it will leave your family unchanged. Challenge
yourself to give emotional leadership to the family.
Sometimes a joke can break the tension. At other
times, the family needs to do something different—
perhaps go somewhere with you. Occasionally a
"family council," where family members openly discuss their feelings, will reveal hidden agendas that
have contributed to the mood of the home. If these
attitudes are not talked out, they may escalate into
severe problems.

Many times, sharing a portion of God's Word with
the family and offering a simple prayer will bring
them back to emotional security. This needs to be
done in a sharing way, not in a preaching manner.
Talk *with* them, not *down* to them.

A FATHER BRINGS STABILITY TO THE HOUSE

Probably the greatest emotional stability the father
can bring into his home is constancy—dependability.

A Father's Role as Provider

There are few constants in the world today. Everything is changing, and this change produces stress and brings confusion to your children and often to your wife. By behavior and attitude, convince them that your love, care, provision, and concern for them are as constant as the sunrise and sunset.

Your Father shows you that. He wrote for our knowledge:

I the Lord do not change.   Malachi 3:6

What He was, He is. What He said, He says. What He did, He does. He is the unchangeable, omnipotent, omniscient, omnipresent, eternal God. This God is your Father. Take lessons from Him. Draw life and energy from Him. As the psalmist assured us:

For this God is our God for ever and ever; He will be our guide even to the end.   Psalm 48:14

He is not only our pattern for constancy, He is also our source of love for the family.

THE NEED FOR A FATHER'S LOVE

Whoever has My commands and obeys them, he is the one who loves Me. He who loves me will be loved by My Father, and I too will love him and show Myself to him.   John 14:21

Two verses later Jesus almost repeated Himself in saying:

If anyone loves Me, he will obey My teaching. My Father will love him, and We will come to him and make Our home with him.   John 14:23

These verses teach that there is a three-way flow of love. When we show our love for Jesus by obeying His teaching, we are assured that the Father loves us, and that Jesus also extends His love to us. This is more than an emotional touch from God. Jesus says that the Father and the Son will make Their home with us. The love They offer is relational.

This is illustrative of the love that should be found in every home. The love of the child invokes the love of the parents. The child is welcomed into the love the parents have one for another. In his introductory remarks in his Ephesian letter, Paul said:

He hath made us accepted in the beloved.
Ephesians 1:6, KJV

J.B. Phillips translates this verse:

He made us welcome in the everlasting love he bears towards the Beloved.

What marvelous security God has offered to us! We are not merely offered God's love; we are welcomed into the abundant love the Father has for Jesus. This is what earthly dads owe to their children. Make your children welcome into the love you have for your wife. Accept them as an extension of, or an addition to, that love.

It is interesting that while the Bible commands us fathers to love our wives, our neighbors, and even our enemies, there is no verse that commands us to love our children. We are told to provide for them, to correct them, and to guide them, but there is no command given to fathers to love their offspring. Some fathers, unfortunately, never do. They feel jealous of, or in competition with, their children for the love and attention the wife gives them.

Paul wrote two implicit commands for us fathers:

The Need for a Father's Love

Fathers, do not exasperate your children; instead, bring them up in the training and instruction of the Lord.   Ephesians 6:4

Fathers, do not embitter your children, or they will become discouraged.   Colossians 3:21

Why did Paul feel it necessary to warn fathers against exasperating their children? (*"Provoke not your children to anger"* is how the King James Version renders it.)

Is it possible that Paul had observed that siring a child does not automatically instill a love in the man for that child? Perhaps Paul was addressing a problem that causes thousands of American men to abandon their wives at the announcement of pregnancy. Other men leave shortly after their child is born.

Unlike the woman who carries the developing baby in her womb, forming an invisible bond that grows stronger month after month, the man is very emotionally removed from the process of birth. It requires an act of his will to get positively involved. Rather than enjoy the process of birth, he is more apt to resent it, for it is an intrusion on his lifestyle. He may become indignant at the lessening of sexual activity, and he might fight feelings of jealousy over the attention his wife gives to the child after she gives birth.

As a pastor, I enjoyed dedicating babies. I often noticed a marked difference in the attitude of the mother from that of the father—especially when it was the first child. The wife was proud and pleased with what their union in marriage had produced, but the husband appeared to feel that the weight of the world had just been placed on his shoulders. He knew that he had lost much of his independence. His boyhood days were over. His selfish nature was being challenged, and he now had to share his wife's time, love, attention, and care with the baby. The baby was an extra expense added to the budget. If the father has been observant, he knows that this expense will only get greater as the child matures.

If this new dad has been taught to accept responsibility, he will make the adjustment to a child in the home. If he hasn't, he may very well walk off or be jealous and resentful of the child. Maybe this is why in both letters mentioned above, Paul prefaced his command to *"provoke not your children"* with the injunction:

> *However, each one of you also must love his wife as he loves himself, and the wife must respect her husband.* Ephesians 5:33

> *Husbands, love your wives and do not be harsh with them.* Colossians 3:19

Although it is true that the greatest gift a dad can

give his children is a warm, open love for his wife, the children also need the expressed love of their father. It is an inclusion of the children into the family love that brought them into the world. When the children are separated from that love with teasing, provoking, or being slighted, they will respond in bitterness, resentment, and anger. It is expressed love that generates love in another. Treat your children lovingly, and they will respond lovingly.

The Bible does not abound with role models of this love, but in the Gospel of John, we read that Jesus spoke of eight things His Father offered to Him while He was here on Earth. The first was an abounding love relationship. From His conception to His crucifixion, Jesus basked in an awareness of His Father's love. God demonstrated that love for Jesus in multitudinous ways and even expressed it vocally from Heaven on two or more occasions. Jesus found security and comfort in His Father's love, and it didn't really matter that some persons hated Him.

THE FATHER'S LOVE FOR JESUS

Jesus said:

For the Father loves the Son and shows Him all He does. Yes, to your amazement He will show Him even greater things than these.   John 5:20

There are at least four factors in the Father's love for Jesus:

1. It was unlimited.
2. It was unconditional.
3. It was unfailing.
4. It was uninhibited.

These are excellent guidelines for fathers today. Times may have changed drastically, but the need for love between fathers and children is as great today as it was in the days of covered wagons.

God's love for Jesus was completely unlimited. God set no boundaries on His love for His Son. From the womb to the tomb, God surrounded Jesus with whatever measure of love was needed. Similarly, we dads need to give all our love to all our children all the time. That we gave lavishly of our love last week does not meet the needs in our children's lives this week. We may have loved them through problem number one, but now they might be living with problem number nine, and our love needs to be so limitless that it will get involved in their current need.

A father's love dare not be like a bank account that can be overdrawn. It should be more like an ocean that can never be drained dry. Your children need to sense that there are absolutely no limits on your love, even though it sometimes must be "tough love." True love is not indulgent, but it *is* inexhaustible.

Similarly, God's love for Jesus was totally unconditional. It was not a return for Jesus' coming as Savior to the world. God just loved Jesus! We dads need to learn this secret. We love our children for who they are, not for what they have done. It is a serious mistake for a father to say to his child, "I'll love you if you make straight A's in school," or, "If you will wash and wax the car, I'll really love you." This conveys a dual message. First, it says that love can be purchased through acceptable behavior. Conversely, it also says that unless our children please us, they will go unloved. Neither should be true. Love your children just because they are your children. Their behavior should never affect your love for them.

It is easy to love the infant asleep in the crib. As your children mature in life, however, their behavior often destroys the image of innocence and cuteness. The more they try to step out on their own, the more likely they are to fail in some areas. Despite the tough front they may put on, they will be inwardly crushed by self-incrimination after failure. They may need discipline, but they desperately need love. They need to know that your love for them does not cease when they fail to meet your expectations. They need a path that leads back to normal living, and your love should be that consistent, available path. Look to Father God as your pattern, and love your children unconditionally.

God's love for Jesus was consistently unfailing. Jesus could count on it day or night. There are times when we dads feel especially loving, but our children need our expressed love even when our circumstances are threatening and our emotions are drained. The ups and downs of our jobs should not influence our love for our children or its consistent expression. When we are facing extremely negative circumstances, our children feel the tension in the home. They can easily interpret this as rejection. Ask God to help you flow unfailing love to your children no matter what your circumstances may be.

God also loved Jesus with uninhibited love. Six times the New Testament tells us that God spoke from Heaven:

> *This is My Son, whom I love; with Him I am well pleased.*   Matthew 3:17
> Matthew 17:5
> 2 Peter 1:17
> Mark 1:11
> Mark 9:7
> Luke 3:22

God never hid His love for Jesus, even in public. It does wonders for our children when we can honestly praise them and express love for them around other people. It helps build a positive self-image in them. We need not act like doting, bragging grand-parents, but we can uninhibitedly let the world know that we love the children God has entrusted to our care.

We dads are often inhibited in expressing love, for we've associated love with lust. We need God's help to bring our expressions of love for our children into the open. A father can express more love to his son or daughter in a ten-second hug than he could in a ten-minute discussion. We need to be able to touch, kiss, and hug our children, and openly say, "I love you." It releases our emotions, and it stabilizes and strengthens the lives of our children as well.

Maybe a father doesn't automatically love his children, but he can learn to love them. His love is an act of his will before it is a release of his feelings. But this means that his love will be rock solid and consistent. May God help us dads to constantly undergird our homes with love. Where our love may be weak, we have access to God's love, which is strong and limitless. Jesus said:

As the Father has loved Me, so have I loved you.
Now remain in My love. John 15:9

We dads must give God's love to our children in the same way we have received it.

There are, of course, fathers who yearn to have children. They rejoice when they discover that their wives are pregnant, and they emotionally walk through the pregnancy with them. They brag to their fellow workers that they are about to become a father, and some of them actually buy toys for their expected son or daughter.

The birth of a child is often a time of great celebration for the father. Gifts are given to others. Phone calls are made to friends and relatives announcing the arrival of the baby, and flowers are sent to the mother in the hospital. How fortunate is the child who was wanted and received by the father even before the day of birth! That is exactly what God did to us. He loved us long before we were born. David said:

> *From birth I was cast upon You; from my mother's womb You have been my God.* Psalm 22:10

God chose to bring us unto Himself. Many fathers have done the same thing.

There are at least five things we can notice about a father's love for his offspring:

1. Father's love is expected.
2. Father's love is exhilarative.
3. Father's love is expandable.
4. Father's love is exemplary.
5. Father's love is exotic.

These should be consistent qualities in the lives

of any father. They are, you realize, unvarying characteristics in God's love for those of us, who are His sons. And God is our ultimate role model.

FATHER'S LOVE IS EXPECTED

As we have already noted, the Bible does not command fathers to love their children, but it does expect them to. Perhaps as God made us, a father's love is so innate that it need not be commanded. How can a father take his infant child in his arms for the first time without having a surge of love rise in him? He may feel awkward and he may act embarrassed, but love flows from him to his baby.

An unloving father is unnatural. He is an abnormality, functioning contrary to nature. Unfortunately, in our society this deviant behavior can be seen in homosexuality, abandonment of children, and child abuse. These are the patterns that make the evening news, but for every depraved dad mentioned in the news, there are thousands of faithful fathers extending their love to their children. I see them in airports and I watch them in church. They give the children the love that is expected of fathers. They measure up to God's standards pretty well. None is perfect, but love covers those imperfections.

FATHER'S LOVE IS EXHILARATIVE

Few things can enliven or stimulate children the

way an expression of love from Daddy can. Just the sound of his car turning into the driveway can elicit joyful shouts of "Daddy's home!" The competition for attention at the front door is accompanied by happy yelling while each child tries to out-talk the others to tell Daddy something important that happened that day.

Picking up the youngest child while bending down to hug the others, the father feels like a king being welcomed back from a victorious war campaign. He may feel that this is the normal mood of the home, but mother knows better than that. Sometimes my wife used to fret that the children, who had been whining and complaining, could so come alive and be happy just because Daddy walked in.

The father is not around the house all the time. He is not involved in the hour-by-hour rules of the home or its humdrum activities. He is often seen as the exception to the rules. He is "mister excitement" to the children. He is the exhilarative force of the home.

When the father takes time to play ball with his sons or play dolls with his young daughters, it is excitement time. Even his careful listening to what the children have to say can enliven their lives. Showing an interest in their school activities, attending a function they are involved in, or examining an art project they have brought home and giving it a place of prominence in the house can bring a level of cheer to the children, and often to the entire home, that is far higher than normal.

Since children learn so much about living by playing games, they delight in having Daddy join them in this world of make-believe. Any board game on the market is much more fun to play when Daddy plays it with them. It doesn't matter that they continuously change the rules of the game to their advantage. They're having fun playing with their father.

Sometimes we fathers forget how small a world our children live in. When we invite them into our world by taking them with us, we not only enlarge their knowledge, we also increase their joy of living. As we introduce them to our associates and friends, their world is broadened, and their hearts fill with pride and joy as we say, "This is my son," or, "This is my daughter." It takes so little to increase the joy of our children. A father's love demonstrated in many little ways stimulates the children to positive responses in life.

FATHER'S LOVE IS EXPANDABLE

We see this principle beautifully demonstrated in Father God. That He loved Jesus is obvious, and His love for you and me is clearly declared in the Bible. *"For God so loved the world..."* (John 3:16). God expanded His love to include more and more people. Since we love with God's love, our love is equally expandable. You pledged all your love to your wife when you married her. When the first baby arrived, you found it possible to expand that love to include the infant. Amazingly, your love has been capable of expansion to include every child who came to share your life.

In some cultures, the father welcomes a son into his love, but totally rejects a daughter. Even in our American culture, it is not so unusual for a father to have a favorite child and one he rejects. In the Old Testament, Abraham was such a father. He totally rejected Ishmael, his firstborn son, after the birth of Isaac. It caused such conflict in the home that Abraham finally expelled Ishmael and his mother from the house. What a pathetic example of parenthood! It induced an anger that still causes the world pain, and engenders warfare in the continuous conflict between the Arabs and the Jews, descended from Ishmael and Isaac respectively.

You may have a child who responds to you more warmly than the other children, or you may understand one of the children better than the others, but each child should equally share your love. The love you offer as a father can, and must, expand to include every member of your family.

FATHER'S LOVE IS EXEMPLARY

Some things can be taught with rules, and other

things are learned from books, but love is best learned by seeing it demonstrated. In His final discourse with His disciples before His crucifixion, Jesus told them:

A new command I give you: Love one another. As I have loved you, so you must love one another. John 13:34

Christ did not rely exclusively on a commandment. He leaned heavily on an example: *"As I have loved you, so you must love one another."*

The same principle applies in your home. You can hardly expect your children to love one another if they don't have an example of love from you. If you show little respect to your wife, it will be difficult to teach your children to respect her. If you keep your love locked up inside you, you can't expect your children to be openly warm and loving in the home.

You may not like this responsibility, but the naked truth is that you are more an example of love than an enforcer of it. You can compel behavior patterns, but you cannot force emotions. These must be induced by a powerful example. What you do is more forceful than what you say.

I am not unaware of the inherent differences in personalities. Some men can gush love emotionally with hugs, kisses, and loving words, while to other fathers this is unnatural. But love is expressible in every personality. Be yourself. Be your loving self. Your children know your personality better than anyone else in the world. The important thing is to release your love in demonstrative ways so your children know that they are loved by their father.

A father's love is far more exemplary, especially to sons, than is the mother's. Somehow, a mother's love is taken for granted, but a father's love is embraced as a gift. Consistently give your child the gift of your love. It is fulfilling, rewarding, and an example of how they should show love to others. The measure and manner of your expressed love will deeply affect relationships in their own marriages in the future; the way they relate to their spouse and children will be influenced by the way you love them now.

FATHER'S LOVE IS EXOTIC

The dictionary defines exotic as: "(1) that which is introduced from another country; (2) strikingly different or unusual." [9] I believe that a father's love fits both of these definitions.

Most of us fathers lack sufficient inherent love. We need to import it from "another country." Fortunately for us, Heaven has more love than we can use in two lifetimes. In His high priestly prayer, Jesus told the Father:

The Need for a Father's Love

I have made You known to them, and will con-
tinue to make You known in order that the love
You have for Me may be in them and that I My-
self may be in them.   John 17:26

Jesus provided that the Father's love might be in us, just as He took up residence in our lives. We, then, are able to love our children with an "exotic love," a love that comes from another country—Heaven.

All the characteristics of God's love for Jesus, and subsequently for us, are far superior to the natural love a father has for his offspring. At the beginning of this chapter I said that God's love for Jesus was unlimited, unconditional, unfailing, and uninhibited. Dad, that love is available to you to extend to your children. You don't have to develop it. Just receive it and release it.

"Exotic" also means "that which is strikingly different or unusual." That characterizes a father's love. Dad, you love your children in a way that is far different from the way anyone else loves them. Mother's love is life-giving. The love of grandparents is nourishing, but the father's love is stabilizing and sustaining. No amount of love from others can replace the love of a father.

Dad, reach heavenward and touch the love of Almighty God for your life and for the lives of your children. Let His exotic love fill your life and the lives of your children as it flows through you. When your patience has been tried to the limit, reach for God's unlimited love. If you wonder how you can continue to love your children after what they have just done, let God's unconditional love flow through you to them.

Sometimes the pressures of your job and of life in general seem to drain you of all emotion. That's when you need to let the unfailing love of God overwhelm your soul until you find comfort and strength in pouring out that love on your children.

Similarly, when you find it difficult to express your love to your family, let God's uninhibited love flow directly through you to them. As you let Him hug you, return the hug to your own children. As you see Him rejoicing over you, rejoice over your children with the same measure of joy. You have access to a strikingly different or unusual love for your family. It is the love of God, and you are the major channel God intends to use to flow that love into your home. When we learn to channel love to our children, we will easily take the next step and offer approval to them.

TEN

THE NEED FOR A FATHER'S APPROVAL

Jesus replied, "If I glorify myself, my glory means nothing. My Father, whom you claim as your God, is the one who glorifies me.   John 8:54

Significant in the life of Jesus was His awareness of His Father's approval. God the Father praised, extolled, and lauded Jesus. If Jesus, the perfect man, was dependent upon His Father's exaltation, how much more are our children dependent upon the praise and expressed approval of their earthly father? It is fundamental to establishing a positive self-image.

From toddlers to teenagers, children strive to find their self-image. They boast and brag of their abilities. Little ones constantly show what they can do, even if it is little more than turning an imperfect somersault. They are asking for approval, acceptance, and assurance. Because this need is progressive in them, they ask for it over and over again. Children develop so rapidly that they don't really know who they are becoming. They look to their peers and their adult associates for some definition of who they are and of their self-worth in life.

The higher the authority in their lives, the more important the approval becomes to them. When a pastor takes time to express personal approval of a child, an indelible impression is formed. The praise of a school teacher is a powerful ego booster. The ultimate image builder is when you, Dad, take time to express positive approval of them.

Our self-image is very fragile. It is formed bit by bit, and most of these bits come from sources outside ourselves. The more authoritative the source, the more valuable and forceful the input. In most homes the father is viewed as the top authority. This puts added pressure on you, Dad. Although it is true that your children can mature without your approval, they will not be complete in their own personalities. Throughout their lives there will be a vacancy that none other can fill. In seeking to compensate for this lack, they may become overachievers or underachievers. Worse than this, they may turn to stimulants to bolster their sagging egos. Alcohol or drugs may become their support group, or they may turn to gang activity to obtain a sense of self-esteem.

Perhaps it would be profitable to consider at least five levels of a father's approval:

The Need for a Father's Approval

1. Father's disapproval
2. Father's lack of approval
3. Father's approval of the person
4. Father's approval of the performance
5. Father's approval of the maturity

These are somewhat progressive as your child matures, but the principle is the same. Children need their father's approval at all stages of their development.

Although I lost my father more than twenty years ago, I still feel the loss, for he was a great undergirding of my self-image. Many times I have longed to be able to pick up the phone and talk over some of my problems with Dad and hear him assure me that I would come out all right. The greatest thing that Dad could say to me was, "I'm proud of you, son."

Approval and assurance are probably the greatest gifts you can give to your children. Honest praise and compassionate reassurance are marvelous tools for character building in your son or daughter.

FATHER'S DISAPPROVAL

Before looking at your approval, take a look at your disapproval, for there is a positive side to a father's disapproval. A baby comes into this world with no sense of right or wrong. A newborn is totally self-centered. The world revolves around the baby. It is a slow and often painful process to teach a child that we are each merely a part of a larger world, and that there are rules that govern this greater society. It is essential that you progressively move your children from self-centeredness to home-centeredness. This will require education, enforcement, and assurance. Once the rules are known and your children have discovered that these regulations will be enforced, it often takes little more than your obvious disapproval to produce a change in your children's attitude and behavior.

Because your developing children yearn for your approval, your disapproval can be a powerful disciplinary tool. They will respond to your negative reaction because they yearn to be approved and dislike being disapproved. You must, of course, make your disapproval completely understood for this to be effective. You dare not make this a game or they'll out-manipulate you and fail to learn the lesson of obedience.

Do remember, however, that disapproval is somewhat like salt. A little salt will improve the flavor of many foods, but too much salt will make any food inedible. Continuous disapproval can break the spirit of your children. If they do not respond positively to your disapproval, back it up with disciplinary action that will bring them into harmonious obedience to the rules of the home. Follow this with an expression of love.

The Need for a Father's Approval

My father's method of discipline was a switch cut from a branch of a tree. After receiving a thorough switching, I was allowed to go to my room and cry for a while. Then my dad would come in, express his sorrow at the action that had made the switching necessary, and ask me if I was sorry. When I could mutter a sobbing "I'm sorry, Dad," he took me in his arms, kissed me, and assured me of his love. I knew then that I was back in his approval.

There is no age in your children's lives when this disapproval will be totally ineffective. Obviously, as they grow and leave home, your control in their lives will be greatly diminished, but even then your disapproval of their behavior, associates, priorities in life, or the way they handle money will have an effect on them.

We learn in life that we don't have to be totally disagreeable to disagree with one another. You don't make your relationship with your mature children dependent on their pleasing you, but it will become obvious that your relationship would be warmer if the two of you could walk in agreement.

FATHER'S LACK OF APPROVAL

Sometimes a father doesn't exactly express his disapproval; he merely fails to give any approval. Reaching into my memory, I can't count how many people I have counseled who blamed their personality disorders on their failure to gain their father's approval. They tried so hard, but they always seemed to be unsuccessful. For the rest of their lives they majored in gaining the approval of key people, sometimes functioning as self-appointed servants to them; at other times trying to purchase approval with gifts.

I remember a father who so yearned for a son that when a daughter was born, he ignored her and pretended that she didn't exist. She never knew a kind word from her father during her developing years. He never showed her love, and never saw anything in her worth praising.

That young woman matured with a damaged self-image and a very weak image of men. If any male showed her attention, she often responded to him by trading sexual favors for words of love and what she interpreted as acceptance. When she discovered that she had been used as a plaything and then thrown aside, she was even more damaged in her self-image.

Similarly, I remember counseling a man with a very weak self-image. His father was disappointed in him and rejected him because he was "different." The father was an athlete, but the son was a musician, and the father could not, or would not, relate to him. This father's image of manhood would not expand to include his son's image and this disapproval marked the son for life.

The Need for a Father's Approval

Dad, don't reject the child who is born to you. Your child didn't ask to come into this world; you brought the baby into the world. Who knows what your son or daughter could become with a little support and approval from you?

FATHER'S APPROVAL OF THE PERSON

In his sermon on the Day of Pentecost, Peter described Jesus as *"a man approved of God."*

> *Ye men of Israel, hear these words; Jesus of Nazareth, a man approved of God among you by miracles and wonders and signs, which God did by Him in the midst of you, as ye yourselves also know.* Acts 2:22, KJV

Jesus lived and ministered with the consistent approval of His Father. What did it matter that the religious authorities rejected Him? Father approved, and He had come to do the will of His Father.

Suppose for a moment that Jesus had been unaware of His Father's approval. Could He have so successfully endured the taunts of the scribes and Pharisees? Would He have maintained His sense of destiny when it seemed that everyone was forsaking Him? Jesus dared not rely on the feedback of people, for their attitudes toward Him vacillated with what He was currently doing and teaching. He needed the approval of the highest authority in His life–His Father–and He had it. On repeated occasions, God the Father publicly reassured Jesus of Their relationship, and of His ultimate approval of Jesus' actions.

The same principle applies to your children. They desperately need the approval of their father. As I write this chapter, I am ministering in a church in Warren, Michigan. At lunch today, the pastor told me that he phones his father at least twice a week. He was, for a time, an assistant pastor under his father. He said that he needs his father's continued input and approval of what he is doing in the church. This man is now a father and a very successful pastor, but he still desires the approval of his father to maintain an inner sense of balance and well-being.

Perhaps you don't realize it, but you substantially create the self-image with which your children will live. Children who hear their father consistently say, "You'll never amount to anything," seldom do amount to anything. If you tell your son that he is "dumb," he will likely have learning disabilities most of his life. If you tell your daughter that she is "worthless" or "trash," she may very well fulfill your description of her.

Because we are the trainers of our children, we tend to keep an eye open to the weaknesses and failures in their lives. We speak often of the areas in their lives that need changing, strengthening, or improving, without commending them for the areas of strength they do possess.

Recently, I was watching a football game on television. A veteran player moved before the football was snapped and cost his team a five-yard penalty that proved disastrous for that drive. The cameras focused on the coach as he threw off his headset, flailed his arms, and said something we were glad could not be heard. One commentator said, "That player is really going to get hell from the coach when he goes to the sidelines."

The second commentator, who played professional football, said, "I don't think so. The coach knows that this player has been involved in almost every defensive play in this game. He is exhausted and overly anxious to make a big play. The coach won't devastate his ego; he'll compliment how well he has been playing. Maybe tomorrow in practice, he will bring up this failure."

If the second commentator was right, then we fathers could learn a lesson from that coach. Yes, you may be disappointed at your child's failure, but keep it in perspective. Weigh it against your child's successes. Consider the circumstances. The child is aware of the failure, and probably doesn't need to have it pointed out. What's needed is some reassurance that the child has your approval, in spite of that failure.

At a conference, a speaker held up a blank sheet of paper and asked, "What do you see?"

"A piece of paper" was the reply.

He then placed the paper on the podium, made a tiny dot in the center, and held it up again.

"What do you see now?"

"A dot" was the unanimous reply from the audience.

"Imagine this blank paper is a person," the speaker said. "The small dot is the person's biggest fault. The white surrounding the dot represents the total of this person's worthwhile qualities that we so easily fail to see. Often a fault seems bigger than it really is and we allow it to overshadow the many positive aspects of that person's personality." [10]

Dad, keep focused on the piece of paper, not on the black dot. Undergird the person of your child. Help your child develop into a complete and competent individual by your approval. Our lives may have black dots, but the dots are not our lives.

FATHER'S APPROVAL OF THE PERFORMANCE

Your children not only need your approval of them as persons; they will repeatedly turn to you to approve their actions. Playing sports is more fun if the father occasionally plays too. If your child makes the school team, you will add to the joy if you are in the bleachers cheering. As far as possible, your children want to form a partnership or an alliance with you in their activities.

The Need for a Father's Approval

Unlike my brothers, I never went out for sports. Instead, I was on the debate team and in the drama productions at school. These things were not among my father's interests. I cannot remember his ever attending any school activity in which I participated. He died without ever knowing how much his approval of those activities would have meant to me. Etched deeply in my memory is the one time my father attended a contest where I presented a monologue. He had been appointed one of the judges. I was so proud to have him in the front row that I could hardly remember my lines. When I won first place, his hug and congratulations meant far more to me than the award I received.

By the time I became a convention speaker, my dad's health was failing, and it didn't seem worth the effort to come and see me. He was in his final months of life when my first book, *Let Us Praise*, was about ready for release. I secured a copy of the early galleys and flew to his bedside to read it to him. After only two pages he said, "It's too late, son. I'm not interested."

He died without ever expressing approval of my writing ministry. Mother attended some of my conferences and raved about my books, but it never completely compensated for Dad's lack of approval.

I know that you are busy with important things, but take time to be interested in what your children are doing. Give some approval to their performance in life. Find out what is important to your children and, if possible, share your approval with them.

I once sat in the front room of a pastor's home in an important committee session of a convention. The front door opened and the pastor's son walked in. The pastor paused, looked at his watch, and said to the boy, "Thank you for getting in on time as I asked. I really appreciate that."

A big grin stretched across the boy's face as he walked through the room toward his bedroom. The father had taken time in front of guests to express his approval of his son's performance, and it was deeply gratifying to the boy.

Some fathers are pitifully slow to praise their children, fearing that it will make the children sinfully proud. But God praises us, so why shouldn't we praise our children?

When I was a pastor, I taught the parents of my congregation that if they didn't praise their children, they forfeited their right to correct them. Children should not hear only criticism and complaints from us. These negative comments need to be balanced with compliments and commendations.

Of course you will disapprove of poor performance, but also share your approval of acceptable achievement. The report card that contains one low grade may also contain six high marks. Don't speak only of the one failing subject. Approve the good, and see how you can help strengthen the weak area.

The Need for a Father's Approval

Dad, your children don't understand the subtle changes in their bodies. Growth produces awkwardness. They have to adjust to new spatial dimensions. They outgrow their clothes more rapidly than they thought possible. Much of this will be comical to you, but be cautious about laughing at them. If you can laugh with them, excellent, but when a father pokes fun at his children, it usually produces a deep hurt. Help them understand what is happening to them.

Your understanding is especially needed as they go through puberty. The chemical and emotional changes that accompany the body's shift to maturity are all new and somewhat mystical. Be open and honest with your children. Let them know that this is normal and wonderful.

If you are blessed with a daughter, she needs your approval during this time more than any other time in her life. The physical changes occurring in her often damage her self-image. She may visualize herself as an ugly duckling. In comparing herself with other girls her age, she may feel insufficient, or over-developed. She has probably been teased until she isn't sure about herself.

A father's compliments and consistent approval of her developing image will go a long way in helping mature her image of womanhood. If she is considered pretty in the home, she will carry a self-image of beauty with her. Don't let the opinions of the boys in her peer group form her self-esteem. You create her inner sense of beauty with your words of approval and acceptance. She may not have a Miss America face and body, but emphasize her features that are outstanding. Help her learn that true beauty comes from deep within. Show her that posture, attitude, and a smile can overcome any shortcoming that nature may have dealt her. Help her learn that physical beauty may attract attention, but that true inner beauty is what captures the hearts of others.

Help your children in their choice of college and career. Long before they have enough wisdom or experience, your children will be forced to make major decisions that will affect their entire lives. They will choose their college, career, and life's companion while they are very young and idealistic. Help them make these vital choices.

There are countless opportunities available to young people today. Some guidance counseling for career choices is available through the school systems, but dad's opinion counts very high.

Sometimes our children don't know dreams from reality. Although we don't want to destroy their dreams, they often need to be brought back to reality. We need to help them keep their dreams within the realms of achievability. A son who is consistently at the bottom of his math class should not aspire to be an aeronautical engineer. He lacks a fundamental aptitude necessary for that career. Help him rethink his future.

The college your child attends will shape his or her future, and it may very well challenge the fundamental teaching you have given in the home. Help choose a school that will continue to develop your child in body, soul, and spirit. This may require some research on your part.

Your son may pick a school because of its sports program, and your daughter may feel that a certain college is for her because her best friend is enrolling there. Help them recognize better standards for their choices.

Remember, these are not small children to whom you give orders. These are young people who need to have a strong part in the decision. Your role is advisory.

Help your children in their dating. Unfortunately, some fathers know more about their golf partners than they know about the people their sons or daughters are dating. Readjust your schedule so that you have a chance to meet these people. Dad, you know from experience that your son may be moved more by the hormones in his system than by his mind. His thoughts are for the present instead of the future. Help him see what he may be overlooking. A little guidance at this point can save a lot of heartache later on.

If your son or daughter seems to be dating a person you feel would be an acceptable life partner, express your approval. Accept that person into your family. If that person becomes a marriage partner for one of your children, you would rather have a new son or daughter enter the family than have your son or daughter taken from you.

Help your children in their marriages. It is unlikely that your son or daughter will marry a person you feel is really worthy. Probably such a person has yet to be born. However, once the two decide to marry, join the celebration. Let this marriage be an enlargement of the family, not a division of it.

The amount of input you will have in the wedding will probably depend on the closeness you have achieved over the years. Just remember that it is your child's wedding, not yours. Don't try to relive your wedding or provide the things you didn't have at yours. Share your opinion when asked for it and offer suggestions when you feel something is being overlooked. But be an advisor; don't try to be the producer.

In a very practical way, help keep the wedding plans within an established budget. It is sad to see Christians going into deep debt for a wedding. A lavish ceremony doesn't guarantee a lasting marriage. Borrowing against the future to provide an elaborate wedding is a poor beginning for any couple. When they need all the money available for their living expenses, they will be forced to make payments on the past.

As a pastor, I have repeatedly faced the problem of a father's refusing to attend the wedding of his daughter because he disapproved of the man she was marrying. I have always forced the issue and sought to show the father that his real problem was letting go of a girl he deeply loved. He saw the bridegroom as competition to his fatherhood. Don't fall into this trap. A husband is never competition to a father, unless the father sets himself up as a competitor.

For a short season a daughter may withdraw from her father, but very soon she will learn that no matter how much her husband loves her, he cannot fill the place of her father. Similarly, your son may enter marriage with a lot of self-doubt. He will need your approval and assurance. He has watched you fill your role as husband and father, and he will need words of guidance and wisdom as he takes on new roles.

Your approval will be valuable to your children as long as you live. As you move on from being just a father to the enjoyable role of being a grandfather, your approval will be needed more than ever.

A FATHER AS GOD'S SURROGATE

Jesus replied, "If anyone loves Me, he will obey My teaching. My Father will love him, and We will come to him and make Our home with him."
John 14:23

Moses didn't volunteer for his role as the father of Israel. God conscripted him for the task. In trying to convince God that He had made a serious mistake in this choice, Moses insisted that he had been out of Egypt so long (forty years) that he had just about forgotten the language of Egypt. He pled with God:

O Lord, please send someone else to do it.
Exodus 4:13

Angrily, God told Moses that he could use his brother, Aaron, as his interpreter or spokesperson:

He will speak to the people for you, and it will be as if he were your mouth and as if you were God to him.
Exodus 4:16

Moses represented God to Aaron, and Aaron represented Moses to the people and to Pharaoh.

As Moses became the characterization of God to Aaron, so we fathers represent God to our children. It is not that we are qualified for this role; it is simply that we have been chosen to fill it. God didn't give this function to Grandpa, the pastor, or a Sunday school teacher. He vested it in you, Father. And I know that you didn't volunteer for it, anymore than Moses did.

There was one more thing that God told Moses on this occasion:

> *I will help both of you speak and will teach you what to do.*   Exodus 4:15

I believe that this promise is still applicable to fathers who have been chosen to represent God to their children. We need to learn from God what to say and what to do. Jesus challenged us:

> *Take My yoke upon you and learn from Me, for I am gentle and humble in heart, and you will find rest for your souls.*   Matthew 11:29

We fathers need to get into a partnership with Jesus and learn from Him those qualities of God our children need to see in our lives and hear from our lips. We need to learn by close association with Jesus how to be gentle in spirit and humble of heart so we can bring a restful attitude into our homes.

Father, if you rant and rave around the house, your children will associate God more with a thunderstorm than with a sunrise. If you are proud, boastful, and unreachable around your children, they will think of God as arrogant and unapproachable. If, however, you have the tenderness of Jesus, they will find it as natural to talk to God as it is to talk to you. An article in *Christianity Today*, August 27, 1976, reported that family-life specialists Delmer W. Holbrook and his wife had been lecturing and conducting surveys across America. In a survey of hundreds of children, the Holbrooks came up with the three things fathers say most in responding to their kids: "I'm too tired" takes first place; "We don't have enough money" is second; and "Keep quiet" is third.

It is little wonder, then, that prayer has such a low priority in the lives of Christians and church congregations. By associating God with what they see in their home life, people have developed the attitude that God is worn out with His saints, that He lacks the resources to help us, and that He really doesn't want to be bothered anyway. When they go to church they offer God silence, not praise. If petition is directed to God, it is more the begging of a pauper than the request of a child. Father, please don't present this characterization of God to your children.

You stand between God and your children. In that position you fill three related roles:

1. The pattern of God
2. The proxy of God
3. The priest of God

None of these is an easy assignment to fill, but all are necessary roles that God has appointed fathers to fill in their homes.

FATHER, THE PATTERN OF GOD

As the father to so many churches, Paul must have realized his responsibility, for he wrote:

> *Howbeit for this cause I obtained mercy, that in me first Jesus Christ might show forth all longsuffering, for a pattern to them which should hereafter believe on Him to life everlasting.*
>
> 1 Timothy 1:16, KJV

Paul realized that people would see Christ in him and he accepted his role as a pattern of God on Earth. So too must we dads.

As important as it is to be a pattern of manhood and Christian behavior in the home, the most important pattern we fathers become is a pattern of God. At baby dedications, I was accustomed to look the young father in the eye and ask him, "Do you realize that you will be the pattern of God for this baby for the first five or six years of his [or her] life?" This usually shocked the father, and I was rarely given a response beyond a wide-eyed stare.

I explained that for many years, the father would be the highest authority figure in the life of his young children. He would be to them, in their childhood, what God would later become to them in their adult years. The transfer in concept from their earthly father to their heavenly Father would carry the traits of the earthly to the heavenly.

I made the father aware that his children's early teaching about God would present Him as Father. As they are taught to pray, *"Our Father, which art in heaven...,"* their mental image of God will be consistent with their image of their earthly father.

Dad, your children cannot help seeing the Father in Heaven as an extension of their father on Earth. This image often lasts for a lifetime. What an awesome responsibility! Your life needs to present a true picture of God, especially when your children are small. How is your son or daughter going to visualize God after living under your authority for six or seven years? A little verse I memorized in my youth, with slight adaptation to fathers, says:

You are writing a book, a chapter a day,
By the things that you do and the words that
you say.

Your children are reading this book, whether faith-less or true.
Father, what is the gospel according to you?

Unless you have a very close relationship with God and are personally living as exemplary a life as you can, what you say to your children about God will have much of an impact on their lives. Their concept of God is formed by watching you in their very young years. Lifetime decisions are often made very early in life. In a study done several years ago it was learned that more than half of those who became Christian ministers had decided on this vocation by age eleven. Now more than ever before, a father dare not be or do what he does not want his child to be or do. Consistent living, which conforms to what is taught, is now at an all-time-high premium. Therefore it is important that fathers live godly lives in front of their sons and daughters—even when the children are very young.

Your attitude toward God will strongly influence the attitude of your children toward God for many years of their lives. Your children need to see that God is worth a portion of your time. They need to realize that God has a call on your finances. By observation, they will discover whether God is worthy of your worship. These principles may never be discussed with the children, but they are taught by your pattern of response to God. Children will do what they see you do—even when you teach differently than you live.

Since your children will learn so much through observation, and you are their chief demonstrator, their spiritual life will be learned far more through your behavior than through the Bible stories they may learn in Sunday school. If you are active in your church and open about your walk in Christ, your children will develop a positive attitude toward God and the church. It seems natural for children to go to church with their father, but it undermines their trust in you to have to go to church without you.

Few boys want involvement with anything they consider feminine, and anything that Dad doesn't participate in fits that pattern in their minds. When mothers go to church and fathers stay home to watch the ball game on television, a son intuitively associates worship with women. He quickly joins Dad's example of putting pleasure ahead of piety.

Eighteen times the Gospels record Jesus as saying, *"Follow Me!"* His teaching method was demonstration; He was consistently the pattern of behavior He desired in His disciples.

This is the way it must be in the home. When our children are born, we subconsciously say, "Follow me." May we join Paul in saying:

> *Follow my example, as I follow the example of Christ.*   1 Corinthians 11:1

What we fathers often forget is how short a time we have to train our children to face the realities of life. A few short years ago, Albert Siegal wrote in "The Stanford Observer":

> *When it comes to rearing children, every society is only 20 years away from barbarism. Twenty years is all we have to accomplish the task of civilizing the infants who are born into our midst each year. These savages know nothing of our language, our culture, our religion, our values, our customs of interpersonal relations. The infant is totally ignorant about communism, fascism, democracy, civil liberties, the rights of the minority as contrasted with the prerogatives of the majority, respect, decency, honesty, customs, conventions, and manners. The barbarian must be tamed if civilization is to survive.*

We dare not wait until our children are ready for college to instill Christian principles in them. Christian character needs to be made a part of their very nature before they even enter kindergarten.

FATHER, THE PROXY OF GOD

"WANTED," the newspaper ad proclaimed, "a surrogate mother." An infertile woman was seeking a fertile one who would bear a child for her. Press coverage of lawsuits over who has a right to the baby of a "surrogate" mother has made this generation aware of this word. It means "to put in the place of another," or "something that serves as a substitute." Not only can a woman become a surrogate mother for another, as Sarah's maid did in the days of Abraham, but fathers automatically become a surrogate God to their children.

It is serious enough being a pattern of God for the young lives in our homes, but usually it goes beyond this to becoming a proxy for God to the children. We stand in God's stead in their minds. They are unable to produce an image of God, so God uses us fathers to produce it for them. We become surrogates for God.

Jesus came to reveal God to men and women. He accepted the responsibility of being a surrogate image of God while He lived here on Earth. He said:

I and the Father are one.   John 10:30

Anyone who has seen Me has seen the Father. How can you say, "Show us the Father"?
                                        John 14:9

If you knew Me, you would know My Father also.
                                        John 8:19

If anyone loves Me, he will obey My teaching. My

*Father will love him, and We will come to him
and make Our home with him.*   John 14:23

We modern fathers should expect our children to see the image and likeness of Father God in our lives. Although none of us earthly dads has the same relationship with Father God that Jesus had, our children don't know this. To them father is father—whether at the supper table or in church. We are the pattern for God in their lives—whether good or bad.

There are at least four areas where children normally compare their earthly father with the heavenly Father:

1. Reproduction: father as creator
2. Responsibility: father as caretaker
3. Regulation: father as controller
4. Relationship: father as companion

FATHER AS CREATOR:

Children inherently see their fathers as creators. Of course, they don't understand human reproduction as we adults know it, but they have an amazing sense of being the product of Daddy and Mommy. In a looser sense, they believe that Daddy can make or fix anything. He is almost omnipotent in their eyes. This is heady wine for us dads, and we try to maintain this image.

Children are taught in Sunday school that God is

the Creator of this world and everything in it. Child-like faith embraces this, for that is just like Daddy. In the young child's estimation, Dad's making a swing in the backyard is equivalent to God's making the tree the swing hangs on. Each can do the impossible. Each is creative. If Dad never has time to be creative in the child's world, God will likely be seen as able but unwilling.

FATHER AS CARETAKER:

In the matter of responsibility, earthly fathers become surrogates for Father God in the children's understanding. Christian videos, books, and songs portray Father God as the Provider, Protector, and Patron of the children. Almost automatically the children relate to Dad's provision for their lives and project this onto God. They associate the way Daddy protects them with the way Father God will protect them. They project onto God the way their earthly dad accept his responsibility as a special guardian over their lives, as their patron. Daddy becomes a surrogate for God as their caretaker. If the father is irresponsible in caring for his children, God will likely seem very irresponsible too.

FATHER AS CONTROLLER:

When it comes to regulation, the father mimics God from day one of the child's life. Daddy is the lawgiver and enforcer in the home, or at least he should be. He sets goals and limits in the home and enforces them. The child's life is lived within boundaries the father imposes and administers. If this is handled in a shoddy or inconsistent manner, the child will think that Father God is careless and variable. There will be little or no respect for the Word of God or the rules of society. If, on the other hand, Dad rules firmly but lovingly, God will be viewed in the same manner, and obeying His Word will be quite natural to the growing child.

The manner of dad's regulation in the home is as important as the fact that he exercises control. The child quickly learns whether Daddy is a forgiving controller or a retributive one. This concept will be projected onto Father God. The ability to accept divine forgiveness is often traceable to the availability of forgiveness in the home during the early days of childhood. God is viewed as loving or harsh, according to the way the father treated the child in the home. What a responsibility!

FATHER AS COMPANION:

More than likely, the most important model of God we dads present to our children is the kind of relationship we share. Early Christian training of our children urges each child to relate to God as a loving and trusted companion. A child's ability to do this probably depends on what has been demonstrated in the home. Was the father's relationship with the mother a loving relationship or one of arrogance, contempt, and scorn? In the child's mind, that is what he or she can expect out of a relationship with Father God.

What was Dad's relationship with the entire family? Was it selfish, or selfless? Was it greedy, or giving? Was Dad a giver, or a taker? In the child's mind, the father's behavior indicates the way God is.

The father's relationship with his child will shape the child's relationship with God. If Dad is close to the child rather than distant, God will seem intimate. If Dad can touch as well as talk, the child will be open to the closeness of the Spirit of God. The child needs to know that Daddy more than just likes his children; he actually loves them. When love flows in the home, then accepting the love of God will be second nature to the children.

FATHER, THE PRIEST OF GOD

As your children mature, they will see your clay feet and discover your humanity, so they will visualize you less as a surrogate for God and more as a priest of God. This is a biblical pattern for all Christian fathers.

God has consistently related to families. He created and placed Adam and Eve in the garden with this injunction:

Be fruitful and increase in number; fill the earth and subdue it. Genesis 1:28

God planned for families from the very beginning. When, many generations later, God called Abraham, He told him:

No longer will you be called Abram; your name will be Abraham, for I have made you a father of many nations. Genesis 17:5

Slowly, and by natural generation, Abraham increased through Isaac, Jacob, and Joseph to become a mighty nation of families that God brought out of Egypt by their family tribes.

Until the time of Moses, the father of each family was the priest of the home. He offered the sacrifices, made the supplications, and offered thanks to God for the home. Even after the Aaronic priesthood was established for the nation of Israel, God still held the fathers of individual families responsible for the spiritual well-being of the home. It was the father who brought the sacrifices to the Tabernacle in the wilderness. He laid his hands on the head of the sacrificial animal, confessed the sins of the home, and slew the animal before God. The father represented his family in the presence of God and we should do the same.

Although New Testament believers have Jesus as their great High Priest, fathers are still seen as the spiritual head of the home. The primary role of a priest was to create an access to God for others, and to direct their worship toward God. The Old Testament priest brought the people to God, and brought the person of God to the people.

That role has not changed. God still expects you, Dad, to lead your family in praise and thanksgiving to God and in prayers of supplication to God. It is up to you to teach your children to respond to God in a vibrant, faith-filled manner.

Far too frequently in American homes, fathers have abdicated this role, leaving it up to the mother to fill the vacancy. Thank God for praying mothers, but our homes need praying fathers too. Dad, lead your children in prayer and Bible reading every day. Accept your responsibility as the priest of the home. Function as Jacob did when returning home to his parents. We read:

> *So Jacob said to his household and to all who were with him, "Get rid of the foreign gods you have with you, and purify yourselves and change your clothes. Then come, let us go up to Bethel, where I will build an altar to God, who answered me in the day of my distress and who has been with me wherever I have gone."* Genesis 35:2-3

If you don't take the leadership to bring your children into the purposes and provisions of God, it is unlikely that they will ever get there.

Although we Americans are very church-oriented, God views the individual homes as the smallest unit of the church. Remember, Dad, that you have a church in your house and that you are the pastor. Since in the Bible pastors are often called shepherds, accept that picture of yourself, and tend your family with the loving care a shepherd gives to his flock. Feed them, lead them, and protect them. As quickly as possible, bring them into a personal acquaintance with the Great Shepherd, Jesus Christ. That is the ultimate ministry of a priest.

Being a father is an awesome obligation, for it carries with it the responsibility of being a pattern of God, a surrogate for God, and the priest of God for the home. It is true that many false images of God we have projected to our children can be erased through the redemptive grace of Jesus, but why should this be necessary? The indwelling Holy Spirit can enable us dads to demonstrate God's fundamental nature as our Creator, our Caretaker, our Counselor, and our Companion.

Since you cannot escape giving your children their initial image of God, ask the Holy Spirit to teach you how to give your children a proper portrait of God. The older your children get, the more your role as father changes, yet it does not diminish in importance. Sooner than you realize it, you will be a father-in-law and then a proud grandfather. You will continue to need God's help to fill these new roles.

TWELVE

THE ROLE OF FATHER-IN-LAW AND GRANDPARENT

The reason My Father loves Me is that I lay down my life—only to take it up again.   John 10:17

We know that Jesus was speaking of His coming crucifixion and resurrection. Without trying to play God, can't we see an applicable principle here? Our role as father regularly calls for us to lay our lives on the line for our children. We deny our rights and pleasures to give them privileges and joys they would not otherwise have. In the back of our minds often lies the thought that there will come an end to this sacrifice. We look forward to the time our children will marry, leave home, and be on their own.

When that day comes, however, we discover that we have to continue our lives as fathers, to undergird, and underwrite the lives of our young adults. Our role of father, therefore, doesn't cease when our children marry. It merely changes in the way it operates.

I've heard it said, "The trouble with being a parent is that by the time you're experienced, you are usually unemployed." Don't you believe it, Dad! Once a father, always a father. Your role may change, but your relationship doesn't. You are Father to the infant, to the school student, to the college student, to the bride or groom, and you are Father to the brand-new parents. The biggest change in your role is from being their authority figure, while they were in your home, to being their advisor when they leave.

Your goal is to mature your children into accountable adults. There is probably no point at which this ceases, for your maturity level will always be years ahead of theirs. You should prepare yourself to always be counselor, confidant, coach, and collateral for your children—as long as they live. No one should take your place. No one *can* take your place unless you abdicate your role.

However, the relationship you will have with your children after they leave your home will depend on the relationship you developed while they were with you. If you were caring and close while they were in the home, it will carry over after they leave your home. If you were distant and demanding with them when they were children, they may leave home both physically and emotionally scarred.

Assuming that you have enjoyed your children and have made time for them to share in your life, it will be painful for you to let go of them. But as surely as the young bird must leave the nest, so our children must leave the home to begin the cycle of life all over. Often this is done in stages, especially if your child goes to college and lives away from home. The child may be gone until the laundry needs immediate attention, and then come home for a brief season to recuperate in a variety of ways. The visits will get fewer and fewer and be shorter and shorter as the child builds a life away from home.

Eventually the day you both looked forward to, or perhaps dreaded, will come. You'll be introduced to the person your offspring has chosen as a life partner. Wedding bells will soon be ringing, and you will pass your authority to another.

If you have a son, you've done your best to make him as much of a man as possible. Now it requires a woman from among his peers to complete that process. It is amazing how marriage can mature a boy into a man. You will have to trust your years of training, for your son has chosen to accept the ultimate responsibility of adulthood—marriage. He has also chosen to inflict upon you one of your most difficult roles in life—that of father-in-law.

FATHER, THE IN-LAW

Jesus said:

I am the true vine, and My Father is the gardener.
John 15:1

Surely this implies continued fruitfulness. The vine doesn't produce a single crop of grapes. It offers annual crops, but this requires cross-pollination and sometimes even grafting of fresh stock onto the old stock.

Your family needs the same thing. Your son must go outside your family to find his life's companion, just as your daughter cannot marry one of her brothers. It takes two streams of life flowing together to maintain life. This cross-pollination, or grafting, affects not only the new generation, but also the older generation. Things are never the same after the wedding.

Earlier we looked at a few principles that can help your child through the wedding ceremony. Now let's look at a few principles that can help you through this celebration of life. Perhaps, for the sake of brevity, we can look at just three changes that will be demanded of you in your new role:

1. That you accept an enlarged family
2. That you accept limited authority
3. That you accept financial pressure

Your continued relationship with your son or daughter may very well depend on how well you are able to accept these major changes in your life.

ACCEPTING AN ENLARGED FAMILY:
The most obvious of these changes is the need to

accept an enlarged family. You learned to move over and to expand whenever another baby came into your family, but marriage addition to the family is quite different. This newcomer is not the product of your love for your wife. It is your own child's love that is bringing this new person into the family. This person is not the moldable lump of clay that your wife birthed into your family some years ago. This entry into your life is a developed adult.

This intruder has likely been raised in a home quite different from your own. There may be little in common between you, except your common love for your child. You will be forced to get to know a total stranger and accept this person into the hallowed halls of your home.

It takes some doing to make it work. A lavish dinner at a restaurant won't do it. It will take repeated contacts, extended love, and inexhaustible patience. You are not only trying to accept this person, but this newest addition to your home is determining whether to accept you as well. You have a sales job on your hands, and you are both the salesman and the product to be sold.

Remember that lasting relationships are made up of many parts fitted together and cemented with love. It is not unlike a jigsaw puzzle. Keep working at it. It will come together if you give it sufficient time and effort. Don't treat it lightly. Your future relationships with your grandchildren may depend on how well you succeed in integrating this in-law into your family.

Not only are you striving to gain a son or daughter (rather than lose one), you are inheriting a relationship with another set of parents and another family. If they live in the same community with you, this will be a long-term relationship that may develop into an intimate friendship. If they live some distance away, it is possible that after the wedding you will be only Christmas card friends. Never forget, however, that these people have become the mother- and father-in-law to your child, just as you have become the father-in-law to their child. Open your arms to receive them into your fellowship—for the sake of your child.

ACCEPTING LIMITED AUTHORITY:

A second change you will be forced to make is that of accepting limited authority in the life of your son or daughter. You should still have input, but you have no enforcement. Remember that your son or daughter has developed individual views and very much wants to try out some new ideas in life. There are times that, even though you know the new couple are making a mistake, you can do nothing more than share your views, and then stand back and let them make their own decisions.

It probably will be more than your view of life versus their view. The father-in-law on the other side of the family may be offering advice as well.

Furthermore, since the women of this generation have declared equality with the men, there may be quite a few different opinions: the husband's, the wife's, and the two in-laws'. You and I know that your opinion is the superior one, but the children may not see this. Speak your piece in love and then back off. You have no authority to enforce your views.

You may discover, as I have, that our children are not as stupid and naive as we thought. The years of training we drilled into them comes to the surface as naturally as cream rises on fresh milk. They may do things differently than we do, but they may do them well. Different is not necessarily inferior; it is just different. Let them develop their own way of facing life. They are probably going to do it their way anyway. If we don't resist it too loudly, we can maintain a loving relationship without tension or guilt.

ACCEPTING FINANCIAL PRESSURE:

A third change is the need for us fathers to accept financial pressure as a norm for a father-in-law. The cost of living today makes it very difficult for a young couple to get started in life, and they need the help of their parents. This has always been true. Back when we were an agrarian culture, parents often fenced off a section of their farm for the young married couple, and the newlyweds sometimes lived in a back section of the main farmhouse for several years.

This practice would not fit our monetary society, but the principle is the same. Dad needs to share part of what he has gathered to give his children a chance to get started. Do it with great grace, Dad. Don't make your children debtors to you. Let them be recipients of your grace and goodness. Give without strings of control attached.

Usually a gift to get started is only the beginning of the financial pressure you face as a father-in-law. In the early years of marriage, there will be emergencies and unexpected expenses for which the new couple will need your help. You will constantly be faced with the question of whether you are doing them a true favor in bailing them out. Sometimes pressure is a great instructor. Perhaps your child needs to face the consequences of financial irresponsibility. Reaching for your checkbook may hinder learning. At other times your checkbook is like a life raft to a person who has fallen overboard in the ocean.

You will need guidance from God to know what to do. By now you surely have discovered that He is a wise counselor. He understands what is going on in the heart and mind of your child, and it's probable that you don't. If you have brought God into your finances, by this time you have learned to fol-

low the little checks and nudges of the indwelling
Spirit of God.

FATHER, THE GRANDPA

As we have given life to our children, so they, in
turn, produce children of their own. We then become
grandparents and we live on in those grandchildren.
It is sometimes shocking to see so much of ourselves
in our grandchildren. Frequently our grandchildren
are more like us than our own children were.

Someone, obviously a grandparent, wrote,
"Grandparents are God's favorite people. He gives
them children to love and grandchildren to love
them back." As far back as I can remember, preachers have used the cliché "God doesn't have any
grandchildren." I know that they are emphasizing
that all must be born again as individuals, that no
one inherits salvation by natural genetics. Still, is not
Jesus God's *one and only Son* (John 3:16)? In a sense,
then, the rest of us are the progeny of Jesus. If so,
wouldn't that make us grandchildren of God?

Far beyond the theological implications of this, I
hope God does have grandchildren, for they so fulfill our lives. As one father said, "If I had known
grandchildren were this much fun, I would have had
them instead of my children."

Grandchildren trigger our faith in immortality.
Just about the time our bodies begin to argue with

the commands given by the mind, when we prefer to sit and watch rather than participate in activities, a grandchild is placed in our arms. The child looks a little like us, and shows some behavioral traits like ours, and we realize that we are beginning to live anew in our grandchildren. Our time slot on Earth may seem to be very short, but before we exit this life we are often allowed to see ourselves living on in a third generation. This can be awesome, inspiring, or seriously challenging.

Perhaps we should have seen this immortality in our own children, but most of us were so busy caring for their physical needs, training them in their behavior, and getting them educated that we hardly had time to appreciate them as an extension of ourselves. We saw them as a responsibility and sometimes even viewed them as burdens.

It's different with grandchildren. Generally the day-to-day instruction is not our responsibility as grandparents. When we are with our grandchildren, it's a special occasion. We are viewed as great heroes and become the instant object of their love. It is almost impossible to not respond with an outflow of love in return.

By the time we are grandparents, we are far more comfortable with our role in life than when our own children were born. We are less inhibited and find it far easier to express love to the grandchildren than we did to our own children. Hugs, kisses, and special gifts as expressions of love all seem to flow naturally from the heart of grandparents. It is a fun street with two-way traffic, for grandchildren respond joyfully to this affection and attention.

Frequently, by the time grandchildren come into our lives, we are retired with time on our hands, some money in the bank, and aging bodies with minimal ambition to drive them. Enter the grandchildren with their enthusiasm for life. They don't know anything about physical limitations, and they begin to make demands on us that stir youthful attitudes. It is hard to "think old" when we are with our grandchildren. They force a youthful spirit on us that enhances our enjoyment of life. They remind us of the old maxim, "If you want to stay young, be around young people. If you want to die young, try to keep up with them."

Grandparents often play a substitute role in the home. Father and mother sometimes work long hours to maintain a standard of living they want their children to enjoy. This may give them little time to spend with their children. Dr. James Dobson wrote:

A team of researchers wanted to learn how much time middle-class fathers spend playing and interacting with their small children. First, they asked a group of fathers to estimate the time spent with their one-year-old youngsters each day, and received an average reply of fifteen to twenty minutes. To verify these claims, the investigators attached microphones to the shirts of small children for the purpose of recording actual parental verbalization. The results of this study are shocking. The average amount of time spent by these middle-class fathers with their small children was thirty-seven seconds per day! Their direct interaction was limited to 2.7 encounters daily, lasting ten to fifteen seconds each! That, so it seems, represents the contribution of fatherhood for millions of America's children. [11]

Here is where you, Grandpa, come in. Life probably is not pressing on you as hard as it is pressing on your adult child. Use some of your spare time to share with your grandchildren. Fill the spot that has been left vacant by the father's preoccupation with earning a living.

We grandpas have a thousand opportunities to give. We are the child's link to the past. In the uncertainty of today's rapidly changing society, grandparents can be an emotional anchor for the grandchildren. We can help them to understand the scriptural teaching:

What has been will be again, what has been done will be done again; there is nothing new under the sun.   Ecclesiastes 1:9

Technology is changing rapidly, but the foundations of life and the goals of people don't change that much.

Maybe the greatest gift we can give to our grandchildren is a knowledge of God and His Word. If your grandchildren have Christian parents, you are truly blessed. Please remember that, as the grandparent, you have an awesome authority in the eyes of your grandchildren. Reinforce the Bible principles your children are teaching them. Undergird your grandchildren with times of Bible reading and praying with them.

If your children are not actively serving the Lord, they may be totally neglecting the spiritual life of your grandchildren. Nagging your children won't help. Pick up the responsibility as the grandparent, and when you are with your grandchildren, share the wonderful truths of God with them. You don't need to be a professor of theology in a seminary to have something to share. Remember that no matter how little you know about God, it is far more than your grandchildren know. Pass the knowledge of God and His grace from one generation to the next.

Throughout the Old Testament, God made covenants with individuals. I find it interesting that He never made a covenant for a single generation. The major covenants were three-generation covenants. The promises were given to *"you, your children, and your children's children,"* or *"to you, your sons, and your sons' sons."* A major role of grandparenting is to hold our grandchildren in our covenants with God. Just as we held our children before God in faith, that He would bring them into the same walk with Him that we had achieved, so we can hold our grandchildren in the promises into which God has brought us.

This is accomplished far more through prayer than through preaching. Mention your grandchildren by name every time you have a prayer session. Remind God that Heaven will be less pleasant if you are not surrounded there by your children and grandchildren. Talk to God about your grandchildren, and talk to your grandchildren about God. Eventually you will get them together.

If God has no grandchildren, then He is missing out on a great pleasure He has made available to us. What magnitude, what benevolence, what blessing He has bestowed upon us aging ones!

CONCLUSION

Dad, you have an awesome role to fill. Your responsibility to the children you have sired will follow you to the grave. On some men this responsibility rests lightly. They enjoy reliving their lives through their children. For other men, though, the weight of raising children is crushing. The sense of responsibility, the fear of failure, and the lack of understanding of how to be a good father takes all the joy out of fatherhood.

Rather than looking inward for understanding and strength, look upward. God was the one perfect Father, and throughout the Gospel of John, we see repeatedly how He related to His Son, Jesus. He, then, is both the perfect example and the source of our guidance and strength. The New Testament promises us:

> *If any of you lacks wisdom, he should ask God, who gives generously to all without finding fault, and it will be given to him.* James 1:5

Technology is increasing and expanding at a pace that defies even a vivid imagination. You may feel very unqualified to give proper guidance to your child, but God is far ahead of coming technology. Ask Him for wisdom and understanding. You and He can bring your children into a balanced maturity that will enable them to become quality parents who give you wonderful grandchildren to boast about.

END NOTES

1. *The World Almanac and Book of Facts* 1995,(Funk & Wagnall's Corporation) Mahwah, NJ: 957, 960.
2. *The Bible Illustrator*, (Collins Road, NE; Cedar Rapids, IA: Parsons Technology.
3. Ibid
4. Ibid
5. Ibid
6. Ibid
7. Idid
8. Ibid
9. *Webster's Seventh New Collegiate Dictionary*, Springfield, MA: G. & C. Merriam Company 1972.
10. *The Bible Illustrator*, (Collins Road, NE; Cedar Rapids, IA: Parsons Technology.
11. Ibid

- *Notes* -

- *Notes* -

- Notes -